Google Sheets for Beginners

A Step-by-Step Guide to Master the Power of Collaboration, Analysis, and Visualization with Google's Powerful Spreadsheet Tool

Tim A. Kirksey

Copyright © 2023 Tim A. Kirksey

All rights reserved. No part of this publication may be reproduced, distributed, or transmitted in any form or by any means, including photocopying, recording, or other electronic or mechanical methods, without the prior written permission of the publisher, except in the case of brief quotations embodied in critical reviews and certain other noncommercial uses permitted by copyright law.

Limit of Liability/Disclaimer of Warranty: While the publisher and author have used their best efforts in preparing this book, they make no representations or warranties with respect to the accuracy or completeness of the contents of this book and specifically disclaim any implied warranties of merchantability or fitness for a particular purpose. No warranty may be created or extended by sales representatives or written sales materials. The advice and strategies contained herein may not be suitable for your situation. You should consult with a professional where appropriate. Neither the publisher nor author shall be liable for any loss of profit or any other commercial damages, including but not limited to special, incidental, consequential, or other damages.

ISBN-13: 979-8861838870

DEDICATION

To every one of my readers!

TABLE OF CONTENT

INTRODUCTION 1

CHAPTER 1: A COMPREHENSIVE GUIDE TO GETTING STARTED 5

   1.1 WHAT IS GOOGLE SHEETS? 5
   1.2 THE BENEFITS OF GOOGLE SHEETS 6
   1.3 A STEP-BY-STEP GUIDE TO CREATING YOUR GOOGLE ACCOUNT 8
   1.4 HOW DO I GET GOOGLE SHEETS? 10
   1.5 MASTERING THE GOOGLE SHEETS INTERFACE 10
   1.6 CREATING YOUR FIRST SPREADSHEET 12
   1.7 NAVIGATING THE GOOGLE SHEETS INTERFACE WITH EASE 13
      1.7.1 The Toolbar 13
      1.7.2 The Menus 13
   1.8 UNDERSTANDING CELLS 14
      1.8.1 Cell Content 14
      1.8.2 How to Select Cells 15
      1.8.3 How to Select Cell Ranges 16
      1.8.4 How to Insert Cell Content 16
      1.8.5 How to Delete Cell Content 16
      1.8.6 Copying and Pasting Cells 17
      1.8.7 Cutting and Pasting Cells 17
      1.8.8 Using the Paste Special Feature 18
      1.8.9 Dragging and Dropping Cells 18
      1.8.10 Using the Fill Handle 19
      1.8.11 Continuing a Series with the Fill Handle 20
   1.9 COLUMN, ROW, AND CELL MODIFICATIONS 21
      1.9.1 Changing the Row's Height 21
      1.9.2 How to Change the Column's Width 22
      1.9.3 How to Auto Size a Column's Width 22
      1.9.4 Modifying All Columns and Rows 23
   1.10 INSERTING, MOVING, AND DELETING COLUMNS AND ROWS 23
      1.10.1 Inserting a Row 24
      1.10.2 Inserting Multiple Rows at Once 24
      1.10.3 Inserting a Column 25
      1.10.4 Moving a Column or Row 25

1.10.5 Deleting a Column or Row 26
1.10.6 Removing the Contents of a Column or Row 26
1.11 MERGING CELLS OR WRAPPING TEXT 27
  1.11.1 Merging Cells 27
  1.11.2 Unmerging Cells 27
  1.11.3 Wrapping Text 28
1.12 FREEZING COLUMNS AND ROWS 29
  1.12.1 How to Freeze a Column 29
  1.12.2 Unfreezing a Column 30
  1.12.3 How to Freeze a Row 30
  1.12.4 Unfreezing a Row 30
1.13 SAFEGUARDING YOUR SPREADSHEET AGAINST ACCIDENTAL AND MALICIOUS CHANGES
.... 31
  1.13.1 Protecting a Google Worksheet 31
  1.13.2 Setting up Notifications 32
  1.13.3 Setting Data Validation 32
1.14 RENAMING A SPREADSHEET 34
1.15 MANUALLY IMPORTING A CSV FILE TO GOOGLE SHEETS 34

CHAPTER 2: EXPLORING BASIC FUNCTIONS AND FORMULAS 37

2.1 UNDERSTANDING FUNCTIONS 37
2.2 THE PARTS OF A FUNCTION 38
  2.2.1 Arguments 38
2.3 HOW TO CREATE A FUNCTION 39
  2.3.1 SUM 39
  2.3.2 COUNT 39
  2.3.3 AVERAGE 39
  2.3.4 MIN 39
  2.3.5 MAX 39
  2.3.6 Using the Functions Button to Create a Function 40
  2.3.7 Manually Creating a Function 40
2.4 USING THE FUNCTION LIST 41
  2.4.1 Accessing the Function List in Google Sheet 42
2.5 UNDERSTANDING THE BASICS OF GOOGLE SHEETS FORMULAS 43
  2.5.1 Cell References 43
    2.5.1.1 Relative Cell Reference 44
    2.5.1.2 Absolute Cell Reference 44
    2.5.1.3 Mixed Cell Reference 44
    2.5.1.4 How to Prevent Cell References from Changing 45

2.5.1.5 Switching Between Relative, Absolute, and Mixed Cell References 45
2.6 DATA RANGES 47
2.7 CONSTANT VALUES 47
    2.7.1 Manually Changing Constant Values 48
    2.8.1 Arithmetic Operators 48
    2.8.2 Comparison Operators 49
    2.8.3 Concatenation Operators 50
    2.8.4 Reference/Formula Operators 51
2.9 OPERATOR PRECEDENCE AND ORDER OF CALCULATIONS 52
    2.9.1 Modifying the Order of Calculation with Brackets 53
2.10 NAMED RANGES 53
    2.10.1 Identifying Your Named Ranges 54
    2.10.2 Naming Convention for Your Data Range 54
2.11 SIMPLE AND COMPLEX FORMULAS 55
    2.11.1 Basic Google Sheet Formulas 55
    2.11.2 Complex Google Sheet Formulas 56
    2.11.3 Tips for Reading Complex Formulas Without Stress 56
2.12 USING LOGICAL FUNCTIONS 57
    2.12.1 OR(), AND(), and NOT() Functions 57
    2.12.2 Using Comparison Operators with Logical Functions 58

CHAPTER 3: SPREADSHEET CUSTOMIZATION AND FORMATTING 61

3.1 FORMATTING CELLS 62
    3.1.1 Modifying the Font 62
    3.1.2 Modifying the Font Size 63
    3.1.3 Adding Underline and Italics to Your Text 63
    3.1.4 Making Your Text Bold 63
    3.1.5 Changing the Text Color 64
3.2 WORKING WITH TEXT ALIGNMENT 65
    3.2.1 Vertical Text Alignment 65
    3.2.2 Horizontal Text Alignment 65
3.3 CUSTOMIZING CELL BORDERS AND FILL (BACKGROUND) COLORS 67
    3.3.1 How to Change the Fill Color 67
    3.3.2 How to Add Cell Borders 67
3.4 CONDITIONAL FORMATTING RULES 68
3.5 MAKING AND FORMATTING A GOOGLE SHEET TABLE 69
    3.5.1 Creating Your First Google Sheets Table 70
    3.5.2 Formatting Your Google Sheets Table 70

3.5.3 The Application of Alternating Row Colors 71
3.5.4 Making a Filtered Table 71
3.5.5 Making Your Table Collapsible 72
3.5.6 How to Group Table Columns 72
3.5.7 Grouping Table Rows 73
3.5.8 Creating a Searchable Table in Google Sheets 73
 3.5.8.1 Giving Your Table a Name 74
 3.5.8.2 Assigning a Name to a Specific Column to Make It Searchable 74
 3.5.8.3 A Working Example of Searching with Columns 74
3.6 MAKING AND FORMATTING CHARTS AND GRAPHS 75
3.6.1 Making a Chart or Graph 75
3.6.2 How to Switch the Type of Chart 75
3.6.3 Changing the Data Range 76
3.6.4 Adding Gridlines 77
 3.6.4.1 Tips and Tricks for Gridlines 77
3.6.5 Customizing Points and Bars on a Chart 78
3.6.6 Changing Your Chart's Font, Background, and Other Features 78
3.6.7 Customizing Chart Titles, Subtitles, and Their Fonts 79
3.6.8 Customizing Chart Legends, such as Color, Style, Font, or Position .. 80
 3.6.8.1 Adding or Editing the Legend Header 80
3.6.9 Working with Chart Items 81
 3.6.9.1 Removing Items from Your Chart 81
 3.6.9.2 Deleting Specific Items 82
 3.6.9.3 Deleting Error Bars or Data Labels 82
 3.6.9.4 Removing Other Items 82
 3.6.9.5 Moving Items on Your Chart 82
 3.6.9.6 Resetting the Location of an Item 83
 3.6.9.7 Resetting the Location of All Items 83
3.6.10 Moving a Chart 83
3.6.11 Resizing a Chart 84
3.6.12 Quickly Navigating Your Charts with Keyboard Shortcuts 84

CHAPTER 4: DATA MANAGEMENT 87

4.1 SORTING AND FILTERING DATA 87
4.1.1 Types of Sorting 88
4.1.2 Sorting a Range 88
4.1.3 Sorting a Sheet 89
4.2 CREATING A FILTER 91
4.2.1 How to Apply More Than One Filter 91

 4.2.2 Creating a Filter View During Collaboration *92*
 4.2.3 Clearing Every Applied Filter *92*
 4.3 DATA VALIDATION 93
  4.3.1 What is Data Validation? *93*
  4.3.2 Using Data Validation *93*
   4.3.2.1 Using Data Validation to Create a Dropdown List 93
   4.3.2.2 Using Data Validation to Set a Number Limit 94
   4.3.2.3 Using Data Validation to Check Dates 96
   4.3.2.4 Using Data Validation with a Custom Formula 97
 4.4 MANAGING AND ORGANIZING YOUR SHEETS AND TABS 99
  4.4.1 Adding a New Tab to Your Spreadsheet *99*
  4.4.2 Renaming a Tab in a Spreadsheet *99*
  4.4.3 Remove a Tab from Your Spreadsheet *100*
  4.4.4 How to Reorder Your Tabs *100*

CHAPTER 5: DATA SHARING AND COLLABORATION 101

 5.1 SHARING WITH SPECIFIC PERSONS 101
 5.2 RESTRICTING ACCESS TO YOUR SPREADSHEET 102
 5.3 UNSHARING A SPREADSHEET FILE 103
 5.4 SHARING A LINK TO YOUR SPREADSHEET 103
 5.5 CHATTING WITH COLLABORATORS IN GOOGLE SHEETS 104
 5.6 DIFFERENT METHODS FOR TRACKING CHANGES IN GOOGLE SHEETS 105
  5.6.1 Using Version History to Track Google Sheet Changes *105*
   5.6.1.1 Restoring from a Previous Version 105
  5.6.2 Enabling Notification Rules to Track Google Sheet Changes *106*
  5.6.3 Using Cell Edit History to Track Changes *106*
 5.7 USING COMMENTS WHILE COLLABORATING IN GOOGLE SHEETS 107
  5.7.1 Adding a Comment to Your Sheet *107*
  5.7.2 How to View a Comment *107*
  5.7.3 Taking Action on a Comment *108*
  5.7.4 Linking, Deleting, and Editing a Comment *108*
  5.7.5 Replying to a Comment *108*
  5.7.6 How to Resolve Your Comment *109*
  5.7.7 How to Use the Comments Sidebar *109*
 5.8 SHARING YOUR SHEETS WITH NON-GMAIL USERS 111

CHAPTER 6: MODERN DATA ANALYSIS METHODS 113

 6.1 DATA ANALYSIS FROM A VARIOUS APPROACH USING PIVOT TABLES 113
 6.2 WHAT ARE PIVOT TABLES? 114

6.2.1 Creating Your First Pivot Table 115
6.2.2 Editing a Pivot Table 116
 6.2.2.1 Relaunching the Pivot Table Editor Panel 116
6.3 CUSTOMIZING YOUR PIVOT TABLE 117
 6.3.1 Changing the Header Name of Your Pivot Table 117
 6.3.2 Sorting and Ordering Rows or Columns 118
6.4 GROUPING PIVOT TABLE DATA TOGETHER 119
 6.4.1 Grouping Rows Together by a Rule 119
 6.4.2 Manual Grouping 119
 6.4.3 Grouping Rows Together by Date or Time 120
 6.4.4 Ungrouping Items in a Pivot Table 120
6.5 FILTERING PIVOT TABLE DATA 120
6.6 HOW TO USE ADVANCED FUNCTIONS FOR DATA ANALYSIS 121
 6.6.1 Advanced Functions in Google Sheets 122
 6.6.2 ABS 122
 6.6.3 SUMIF 123
 6.6.4 VLOOKUP 123
 6.6.5 COUNTIF 123
 6.6.6 HLOOKUP 124
 6.6.7 MATCH and INDEX 124
 6.6.8 AVERAGEIF 124

CHAPTER 7: HARNESSING THE POWER OF MACROS AND SCRIPTS 125

7.1 AUTOMATING TASKS WITH MACROS 125
7.2 RECORDING A MACRO IN A GOOGLE SHEET 126
 7.2.1 Executing a Macro 127
 7.2.2 Using an Earlier Recorded Macro 127
 7.2.3 Viewing Auto-Generated Code for Your Macros 128
7.3 EDITING A MACRO 128
7.4 HOW TO SCHEDULE A MACRO 129
7.5 IMPORTING CUSTOM GOOGLE APP SCRIPT FUNCTIONS 129

CHAPTER 8: TRICKS AND STRATEGIES FOR EFFICIENCY 131

8.1 KEYBOARD SHORTCUTS FOR GOOGLE SHEETS 131
 8.1.1 Common Google Sheet Actions 131
 8.1.2 Shortcuts for Formatting Cells 135
 8.1.3 Navigating a Spreadsheet 139
 8.1.4 Editing Comments and Notes 143

8.1.5 Opening a Menu *144*
8.1.6 Adding or Changing Columns and Rows *147*
8.1.7 Using Formulas *149*

CHAPTER 9: TROUBLESHOOTING COMMON PROBLEMS AND ERRORS 153

9.1 CATEGORIES OF COMMON ISSUES 153
9.1.1 Spreadsheet Crash *153*
9.1.2 Something Went Wrong *154*
9.1.3 A Network Error Has Occurred *154*
9.1.4 Spreadsheet Keeps Loading *154*
9.1.5 Access Denied Message *154*
9.2 BASIC TROUBLESHOOTING ACTIONS 155
9.2.1 Ensuring a Stable Internet Connection *155*
9.2.2 Clearing Cookies and Cache *156*
9.2.3 Using a Different Web Browser *156*
9.2.4 Getting Rid of Unwanted Access *157*
9.2.5 Clearing Chrome's Hosted App Data *157*
9.2.6 Simplifying Your Spreadsheet for Improved Performance *158*
9.2.7 Ensure your Google Workspace storage is Sufficient *160*
9.2.8 Creating a Copy *160*

CONCLUSION 163

Introduction

In the fast-paced digital landscape of today, where effective data management is paramount in both our personal and professional spheres, it is crucial to have a reliable and efficient method for gathering, organizing, and analyzing information. Enter Google Sheets, a sophisticated and versatile tool designed specifically for data organization. Operating in the cloud, Google Sheets offers an array of features and functionalities that make it the go-to choice in such scenarios.

One of the standout advantages of Google Sheets lies in its user-friendly interface. Being a web-based application, it allows users to access their spreadsheets from any computer or smartphone with an internet connection. Gone are the days of downloading and installing additional software; whether you're working on a desktop, laptop, tablet, or even a smartphone, Google Sheets is accessible with just a few clicks.

Collaboration is another key feature that sets Google Sheets apart. Its real-time editing capability enables multiple users to update the same spreadsheet simultaneously, ensuring everyone stays on the same page. This fosters seamless collaboration, making it easier to track changes and updates, ultimately expediting the overall workflow.

Moreover, Google Sheets offers a wide range of functions and formulas, empowering users to perform complex mathematical operations and data analysis. From basic calculations to advanced statistical analysis, these functions enable users to make modifications and extract valuable insights from their data. Additionally, Google Sheets seamlessly integrates with other Google products like Google Docs and Google Forms, enhancing its versatility and usability.

Data visualization is yet another remarkable aspect of Google Sheets. With built-in graphs and charts, users can present their data in visually striking and easily understandable ways. Whether it's scatter plots, line graphs, pie charts, or bar charts, Google Sheets provides a plethora of visualization options to effectively convey data and results.

Furthermore, automation is a powerful feature of Google Sheets. Through its scripting capabilities, users can automate repetitive tasks and streamline their workflow. Whether it's sending email notifications, generating reports, or automatically updating data from external sources, Google Sheets saves time and energy by automating these operations.

When it comes to data management, security is of paramount importance. Google Sheets prioritizes the protection of spreadsheets and data privacy through robust safety measures. With features such as encryption, access control, and two-factor authentication, users can rest assured that their data is secure.

In summary, Google Sheets is a robust and efficient tool for data management. Its security measures, automation capabilities, data visualization features, advanced functionalities, collaborative tools, and accessibility make it an invaluable asset for individuals and businesses alike. Whether you're a project manager, a data analyst, or a student, Google Sheets provides all the necessary features and tools to effectively organize, analyze, and present data. So, don't let the world of data management intimidate you—Google Sheets is here to empower and expedite your data-driven endeavors.

Chapter 1: A Comprehensive Guide to Getting Started

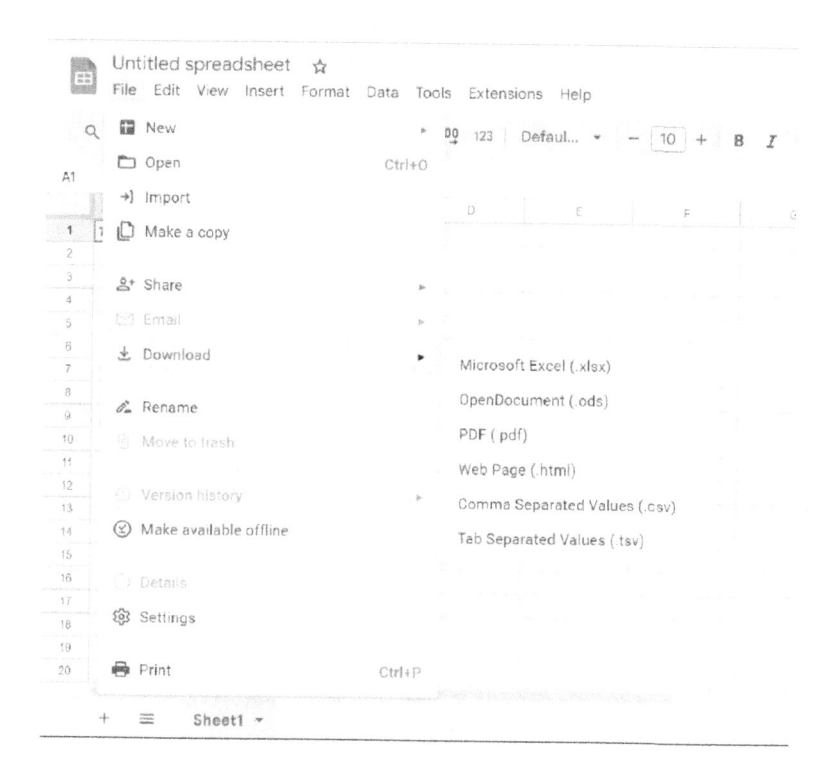

1.1 What is Google Sheets?

Google Sheets, a dynamic spreadsheet application crafted by Google, revolutionizes the way we handle and manipulate data. With its intuitive interface, Google Sheets efficiently arranges information into columns and rows while offering a myriad of mathematical functions to crunch numbers. Since its inception in 2006, this web-based tool has become an indispensable resource for a multitude of tasks.

The versatility of Google Sheets knows no bounds. It serves as a reliable companion for analyzing data, managing vast amounts of information, swiftly inputting data, creating budgetary frameworks, facilitating accounting procedures, and generating captivating visuals and graphs. Furthermore, Google Sheets proves its mettle in data analysis, financial modeling, and even programming, making it an indispensable asset in various domains.

The potential of Google Sheets is limitless, empowering users to accomplish a myriad of tasks effortlessly. Whether you're an analyst, a project manager, or a finance professional, Google Sheets is a powerful ally that streamlines your workflow and amplifies your productivity. Its extensive capabilities go beyond what meets the eye, making it an indispensable tool in the digital era.

1.2 The Benefits of Google Sheets

When it comes to spreadsheet programs, Google Sheets stands out as a versatile and user-friendly option. With its array of features and widespread popularity, it has become a go-to choice for both personal and professional use. Here are some compelling reasons why you should consider incorporating Google Sheets into your workflow:

Ease of Use: Google Sheets prides itself on its simplicity and intuitive interface, making it easy for beginners to learn and navigate. Whether you're a spreadsheet novice or a seasoned pro, you'll find it a breeze to create and manage your data.

Wide Adoption: As one of the most widely used spreadsheet programs in the world, Google Sheets has gained a solid reputation for reliability and compatibility. Its widespread adoption means you can easily collaborate and share documents with colleagues, friends, or family members without compatibility issues.

Versatility: Google Sheets isn't limited to corporate use alone. It seamlessly transitions from the workplace to your personal life, allowing you to create budgets, track expenses, plan events, or even organize your hobbies. The possibilities are endless.

Scalability: One of the standout features of Google Sheets is its high skill ceiling. As you become more proficient, you'll discover the ability to perform advanced calculations, create complex formulas, and automate tasks. This scalability ensures that you can grow and adapt your spreadsheet skills as your needs evolve.

Ongoing Support: Being a product of Google, Sheets benefits from continuous updates and improvements. You can rest assured that any bugs or issues will be promptly addressed, ensuring a smooth and reliable user experience.

Thriving Community: Google Sheets boasts a thriving community of users who actively contribute to its growth and development. Whether you're seeking guidance or looking to share your own expertise, you'll find a wealth of resources and support from fellow users.

Reusability: Another advantage of Google Sheets is the ability to reuse templates and frameworks. This not only saves time but also lowers creation costs. By leveraging existing templates or sharing your own, you can improve your workflow and enhance collaboration.

To sum up, Google Sheets offers an accessible and efficient solution for all your spreadsheet needs. With its user-friendly interface, wide-ranging capabilities, and strong community support, it's no wonder why it has become a popular choice for individuals and businesses alike. Embrace the power of Google Sheets and unlock new possibilities for organizing, analyzing, and sharing your data.

1.3 A Step-by-Step Guide to Creating Your Google Account

To make the most of Google Sheets, it's essential to have a Google account. Fortunately, obtaining one is a straightforward process that won't cost you a dime. To get started, you'll be prompted to provide key details such as your location, birth date, and name. Upon successfully setting up your Google account, you'll be assigned a Gmail email address and a Google+ profile.

If you already have a Gmail address, you automatically have a Google account, so there's no need to go through the hassle of creating a new one. Simply utilize your existing Gmail credentials to access Google Sheets easily.

To create a Google account:

- Creating a Google account is a straightforward process that allows you to access a wide range of Google's services and features. To get started, simply visit the official Google website at www.google.com.

Once there, you'll notice a sign-in button located conveniently in the top-right corner of the page.
- Upon clicking the Sign in button, you'll be directed to a new page where you can create your account. Look for the option that says "Create an account" and click on it. This will bring up a sign-up form that you need to fill out with the required information.
- As part of the sign-up process, you'll be asked to provide your phone number. This is done so that Google can send a verification code to your phone. You'll need to enter this code to complete the sign-up process successfully.
- Once you've entered the verification code and clicked on the Verify button, you'll be taken to a personal information page. Here, you'll need to follow the directions provided and enter details such as your birth date and gender.
- Before finalizing your account creation, it's essential to review Google's Terms of Service and Privacy Policy. Take the time to read through these documents carefully to ensure you understand the guidelines and policies set by Google. Once you've reviewed them, you can proceed by clicking on the "I agree" button.

And that's it! Your Google account has now been created, and you're ready to explore the vast array of services and features that Google has to offer. Enjoy the convenience and benefits that come with having a Google account, and make the most of what the digital world has in store for you.

Quick Tip: When it comes to online services, selecting a robust password is of paramount importance. The goal is to create a password that is not easily guessable by others. Ensuring the security of our online accounts is essential in this digital age.

1.4 How Do I Get Google Sheets?

To get started with Google Sheets, the process is incredibly convenient and accessible. With its web-based nature, you can easily access it from a wide range of browsers and devices. While compatibility spans multiple platforms, Google Chrome, the go-to browser, offers benefits such as the ability to work offline, providing a smooth experience. All you need to do is open your preferred browser and navigate to Google Sheets to begin your journey of seamless spreadsheet management.

1.5 Mastering the Google Sheets Interface

To effectively navigate and manipulate spreadsheets, familiarizing yourself with the Google Sheets interface is essential. This user-friendly platform empowers you to harness the full potential of your data, enabling seamless organization and analysis. By acquainting yourself with the intricacies of this powerful tool, you can unlock a world of possibilities for collaboration, data visualization, and decision-making.

Google Sheets presents a dynamic workspace that facilitates effortless spreadsheet management. Its intuitive design allows for easy access to a wide array of features and functions, empowering users to effortlessly create, edit, and format spreadsheets. Whether you are a beginner or an experienced user, harnessing the capabilities of this interface will undoubtedly amplify your productivity and efficiency.

The interface presents an array of options and tools, neatly arranged to enhance usability. From the familiar toolbar at the top, you can access essential functions such as formatting, inserting formulas, and sorting data. The menus and submenus offer a comprehensive range of options, allowing you to tailor your spreadsheet to meet your specific needs.

The main workspace of Google Sheets is dedicated to displaying your spreadsheet, offering a clean canvas for data input and manipulation. The grid-like structure, consisting of rows and columns, enables seamless organization and categorization of your information. You can easily resize and customize the appearance of cells, rows, and columns to optimize readability and aesthetics.

Collaboration lies at the heart of Google Sheets, and the interface reflects this emphasis on teamwork. Multiple users can simultaneously access and edit a spreadsheet, facilitating real-time collaboration and fostering efficient workflows. The interface provides seamless sharing options, allowing you to grant specific permissions to collaborators and control access to your spreadsheets.

Furthermore, Google Sheets offers a vast library of templates, enabling you to jumpstart your projects with pre-designed layouts for various purposes. From budgeting and project management to data analysis and scheduling, these templates provide a solid foundation that can be customized to suit your unique requirements.

Lastly, by familiarizing yourself with the Google Sheets interface, you gain mastery over a versatile and powerful tool for spreadsheet management. Its intuitive design, comprehensive features, and emphasis on collaboration make it an indispensable asset for individuals and teams alike. So, take the plunge, explore the intricacies of this interface, and unlock the boundless potential of Google Sheets in transforming your data into meaningful insights.

1.6 Creating Your First Spreadsheet

Now that you've mastered the art of accessing Google Sheets, it's time to embark on the journey of creating your very own spreadsheet. Once you find yourself on the main page, a plethora of options await you. You can opt for a blank canvas and let your imagination run wild, choose from an array of pre-designed Google Sheets templates, or venture into the realm of your existing files. The possibilities are endless, and the power to organize, analyze, and visualize your data lies at your fingertips. Let's dive in and unlock the full potential of Google Sheets!

1.7 Navigating the Google Sheets Interface with Ease

Now, we'll explore the features of the Google Sheets spreadsheet editor and learn how to navigate through its interface.

1.7.1 The Toolbar

In the world of software interfaces, the toolbar is a versatile tool for easy navigation. With its array of frequently accessed functions, including the ever-useful formatting options, it serves as a time-saving tool. This intuitive feature will grant you swift access to the tools that you require, eliminating the need for arduous searches and simplifying your workflow. By condensing essential functions into this streamlined command center, you can fearlessly embark on your tasks, knowing that your desired features are just a click away. From formatting text to enhancing the visual appeal of documents, the toolbar empowers you to breeze through your work with unparalleled ease.

1.7.2 The Menus

In Google Sheets, you have convenient access to a plethora of features through its user-friendly menus. Take a look at the 'Insert' menu, which empowers you to easily incorporate cells, functions, charts, or any other objects at your disposal. These menus serve as a way to unlock the full potential of Google Sheets, allowing you to easily enhance your spreadsheets with various elements and functionalities.

1.8 Understanding Cells

In the expansive world of spreadsheets, the building blocks are not just mere rectangles but rather cells that come together to form a complex grid. Each cell, a harmonious fusion of a row and a column, possesses its own unique identity. Columns, distinguished by letters like A, B, and C, stand tall alongside rows, identified by their numerical counterparts 1, 2, and 3.

Every cell claims its spot on the grand stage with a name—a cell address—derived from its row and column coordinates. Consider this scenario: Imagine we choose a cell within a spreadsheet, and suppose this particular cell falls at the intersection of column C and row 10. In such a case, we can denote the address of this cell as C10. It's worth noting that when a cell is selected, the column and row headings surrounding it appear slightly darker, providing a visual cue to its location.

In addition to working with individual cells, you have the capability to manipulate multiple cells simultaneously. This collection of cells is referred to as a cell range. Instead of specifying just one cell, you can indicate a cell range by using the addresses of the first and last cells, with a colon in between. For instance, if you want to include cells C1, C2, C3, C4, and C5 in your selection, you would express it as C1:C5.

1.8.1 Cell Content

When working with spreadsheets, understanding how cell content functions is paramount. A cell, the fundamental building block of a spreadsheet, serves as a repository for a multitude of information. Within each cell, a diverse range of content can be housed, comprising text, formatting attributes, formulas, and functions.

Textual Input
Among the array of possibilities, cells can easily accommodate text, encompassing alphabets, numerical values, and even dates.

Formatting Attributes
Further enhancing the versatility of cells, formatting attributes come into play. These attributes allow for the alteration of the appearance of numbers, letters, and dates. For instance, percentages can be shown as either 15% or 0.15, and the background color of a cell can be easily modified.

Formulas and Functions
The power of cells extends beyond mere text and formatting. They possess the capability to house functions and formulas that facilitate dynamic calculations. Take, for instance, the formula SUM(D3:D9). This formula effectively adds the values of each cell within the designated range (D3 to D9) and then showcases the resulting total in cell D10.

1.8.2 How to Select Cells

When it comes to manipulating cell content, the first step is selecting the cell itself. Take the following steps:

- Simply click on the desired cell to have it selected.
- Once selected, a distinct blue box will encompass the cell, indicating its active state.

Alternatively, you can also make use of the arrow keys on your keyboard to navigate and select cells effortlessly.

1.8.3 How to Select Cell Ranges

When you need to choose multiple cells or a cell range, follow these steps:

- Use your mouse to click and drag, highlighting all the cells you want to select.
- Once the desired cells are highlighted, release the mouse to finalize the selection.

1.8.4 How to Insert Cell Content

When it comes to inserting content into a cell, the process is quite straightforward.

- First, you'll need to select the cell where you want to place the content.
- Once you've done that, simply type in the desired content and press the Enter key.

The content will then appear both in the cell itself and in the formula bar. Alternatively, you can also input and modify cell content directly in the formula bar. It's a simple and efficient way to add information to your spreadsheet.

1.8.5 How to Delete Cell Content

When you need to remove the content of a cell, follow these simple steps:

- Choose the cell you wish to delete.

- Use the Backspace or Delete keys on your keyboard.

This action will effectively erase the contents of the selected cell.

1.8.6 Copying and Pasting Cells

Copying and pasting content into a spreadsheet is a straightforward task that can save you time and effort. Here's how you can duplicate content within your spreadsheet:

- First, select the cells containing the content you wish to copy.
- To copy the selected cells, use the keyboard shortcut Command+C on Mac or Ctrl+C on Windows.
- Now, choose the cell or cells where you want to paste the copied content. You'll notice that the copied cells are outlined with a box.
- To paste the cells, simply press Command+V on Mac or Ctrl+V on Windows on your keyboard.

1.8.7 Cutting and Pasting Cells

When it comes to transferring content between cells in a spreadsheet, cutting and pasting is the way to go. Unlike copying and pasting, which creates duplicates of cell content, cutting and pasting actually moves the content from one cell to another. To execute this action, follow these steps:

- Begin by selecting the desired cells that you wish to cut.

- On a Windows computer, press Ctrl+X, or on a Mac, press Command+X. This keyboard shortcut will cut the cells, but the content will remain in its original location until you paste it elsewhere.
- Next, select the cell or cells where you want to place the cut content.
- To complete the process, press Ctrl+V (Windows) or Command+V (Mac) on your keyboard. This will paste the cells into the new location.

1.8.8 Using the Paste Special Feature

At certain moments, you might find the need to selectively copy and paste specific portions of a cell's content. When faced with such situations, the Paste Special feature comes to your aid.

- To access this functionality, navigate to the toolbar menu.
- Click on the Edit option.
- Next, hover your mouse over the Paste Special command, and a drop-down menu will appear, providing you with a range of paste options to choose from based on your preferences.

1.8.9 Dragging and Dropping Cells

Instead of resorting to the traditional copy-and-paste method, there's a more intuitive way to rearrange the contents of cells: drag and drop. This easy process allows you to seamlessly move cells within your spreadsheet.

- To get started, simply select a cell and position your mouse cursor over one of the outer edges of the highlighted blue box. In a stunning transformation, your cursor will morph into a hand icon, ready to perform its task.
- Now, with a single click, drag the cell to its new destination, easily gliding it across the digital expanse of your spreadsheet.
- Finally, release the mouse button, allowing the cell to settle into its freshly assigned position.

1.8.10 Using the Fill Handle

In certain instances, you may find yourself in need of duplicating the content of a single cell across multiple cells in your spreadsheet. While manually copying and pasting the content into each cell is an option, it can be quite a time-consuming process. Thankfully, there's an efficient trick that can help you accomplish this task with ease.

Allow me to introduce you to the fill handle.

- When you select a cell, a small square, referred to as the fill handle, will make its appearance in the bottom-right corner of the cell.
- By hovering your mouse over this handle, you'll notice that the cursor transforms into a black cross.
- Now, all you have to do is click and drag the fill handle over the cells you wish to populate. As you do so, a dotted black line will enclose the targeted cells.

- Finally, release the mouse button to complete the process, and you will see the selected cells being filled automatically.

1.8.11 Continuing a Series with the Fill Handle

The fill handle serves as a handy tool for extending a series. When working with data that follows a logical progression, such as numerical values or consecutive days, the fill handle takes the guesswork out of the equation. For instance, you can use the fill handle to extend a sequence of dates within a column. With this nifty feature, maintaining the flow of information becomes a seamless task, allowing for smooth data organization and progression.

1.9 Column, Row, and Cell Modifications

Out of the box, each cell in a fresh spreadsheet is uniformly sized. However, once you start populating your spreadsheet with data, you'll find it quite straightforward to tailor the rows and columns to accommodate your specific information.

One can always expect each row and column to be uniformly sized from the very beginning. However, as you delve into the intricacies of spreadsheet manipulation, you will quickly realize that these preset dimensions may not always align optimally with the diverse range of cell content you encounter.

In this section, we will delve into the art of altering the height and width of rows and columns and master the techniques of insertion, relocation, deletion, and freezing. Moreover, we will unravel the secrets of cell wrapping and merging, empowering you to wield complete control over your spreadsheet's layout.

1.9.1 Changing the Row's Height

When it comes to adjusting the height of rows in your spreadsheet, there's a simple method that can provide more breathing room for your cell content. By following these steps, you can effortlessly expand or reduce the row height to suit your needs.

- Position your cursor over the line dividing the two rows. Notice how it transforms into a double arrow.
- Click and drag the row border downwards to increase the height or upwards to decrease it.

- Once you have achieved the desired row height, release the mouse button and enjoy the optimized view of your cell content.

1.9.2 How to Change the Column's Width

To adjust the width of a column in order to display all its content, follow these steps:

- Position your cursor over the line separating two columns until it transforms into a double arrow.
- Click and drag the column border towards the right to expand the column width. Conversely, dragging it to the left will narrow the column.
- Let go of the mouse button once you are content with the new width. This will ensure that all the content within the cells is now completely visible.

1.9.3 How to Auto Size a Column's Width

In order to adjust the width of a column to accommodate its contents, you can take advantage of the auto-sizing functionality. This nifty feature makes it effortless to tailor a column's width accordingly.

Here's how you can do it:

- Position your cursor over the line that separates two adjacent columns. Notice how the cursor transforms into a double arrow.
- Give your mouse a quick double click.
- Voila! The column's width will be automatically adjusted to perfectly match its content.

1.9.4 Modifying All Columns and Rows

In lieu of individually adjusting the size of rows and columns, you can conveniently alter the width and height of all the columns and rows in a spreadsheet simultaneously by employing the Select All button. This method enables you to establish a consistent size for all the rows and columns in the spreadsheet. To illustrate, let's focus on setting a uniform row height.

- Locate the Select All button positioned just below the formula bar and click on it to select all the cells in the spreadsheet.
- Position your cursor over the line that separates two rows. As you do so, the cursor will transform into a double arrow.
- Click and hold the mouse button while dragging the row border to adjust the height according to your preference.
- Let go of the mouse button when you are content with the new row height for the spreadsheet.

1.10 Inserting, Moving, and Deleting Columns and Rows

As you become more acquainted with working on spreadsheets, it's natural to seek ways to enhance your data organization. Whether it's introducing fresh columns or rows, eliminating specific entries, or relocating them within the spreadsheet, these maneuvers can significantly optimize your workflow. Providing flexibility and adaptability, these actions empower you to mold your spreadsheet to your evolving needs.

1.10.1 Inserting a Row

Adding a row to a spreadsheet is a straightforward task. Here's how you can do it easily:

- Begin by right-clicking on the row heading. This action will trigger a drop-down menu to appear, presenting you with two options for adding a row.
- To insert a row above the current one, choose the "Insert 1 above" option. Conversely, if you wish to add a row below the current one, go for the "Insert 1 below" option.
- Once you've made your selection, the new row will automatically appear within the spreadsheet, ready for you to populate with data.

1.10.2 Inserting Multiple Rows at Once

When it comes to adding multiple rows at once,

- Simply navigate to the lower section of your spreadsheet.
- Locate the Add button. This convenient feature allows you to effortlessly expand your spreadsheet by inserting numerous rows at once.

By default, a generous 1,000 new rows will be added with a single click. However, if you desire a specific number of rows, you can easily customize this by inputting your preferred value in the designated text box.

1.10.3 Inserting a Column

Adding a column to your spreadsheet is a straightforward process.

- Simply right-click on the column heading, and a drop-down menu will appear.
- From there, you have two choices for adding a column. You can select "Insert 1 left" to place a column to the left of the current one, or "Insert 1 right" to position it on the right.
- Once you make your selection, the new column will be added to your spreadsheet, ready for you to input data.

1.10.4 Moving a Column or Row

When working with a spreadsheet, you might find it necessary to rearrange rows or columns for easier access to your data. Whether you need to move a row or a column, the process is straightforward. Let's take a look at how to move a column in this example, although moving a row follows the same steps.

- First, select the column that you want to relocate. As you hover your mouse over the column heading, you'll notice that the cursor transforms into a hand icon. This indicates that you can proceed with moving the column.
- Next, click and hold the mouse button while dragging the column to its desired position. As you do this, you'll see an outline of the column,

providing a visual reference for where it will be placed.
- Finally, once you have positioned the column to your satisfaction, release the mouse button. The column will then settle into its new location.

1.10.5 Deleting a Column or Row

Deleting a column or row in your spreadsheet is an easy process. In this example, we will focus on deleting a row, although the same steps can be applied to deleting a column.

- Begin by selecting the specific row you wish to remove.
- Next, right-click on the row heading and choose the option "Delete row" from the available menu.
- As a result, the rows located below the deleted row will adjust accordingly. For instance, if you delete row 9, it will be replaced by row 8.

1.10.6 Removing the Contents of a Column or Row

When it comes to working with data in a spreadsheet, it's crucial to understand the distinction between deleting a column or row and clearing its contents.

- If you aim to clear the content within a column or row without disrupting the arrangement of others, a simple right-click on the heading followed by selecting the "Clear column" or "Clear row" option will achieve the desired result.

1.11 Merging Cells or Wrapping Text

In situations where the amount of information within a cell exceeds its display capacity, alternatives to resizing columns exist. Instead of struggling to fit excessive content into a single cell, two options are available: wrapping the text or merging cells.

Text wrapping adjusts the row height to accommodate multiple lines, ensuring all cell contents are visible. On the other hand, merging allows for the consolidation of a cell with neighboring empty cells, resulting in a spacious single cell for an efficient presentation of data.

1.11.1 Merging Cells

Combining cells is a simple process that can be easily accomplished in just a few steps.

- First, highlight the desired cells you wish to merge, such as the range D1 to F1.
- Next, locate and click on the appropriate button that facilitates the merging of cells.

Once this action is complete, the selected cells will seamlessly merge into a single, unified cell.

1.11.2 Unmerging Cells

To separate a merged cell, simply click on the downward arrow located beside the button for merging cells. From the options presented in the drop-down menu, choose the "Unmerge" option. This will effortlessly disentangle the previously merged cells, allowing you to work with them individually.

1.11.3 Wrapping Text

To wrap up your text,

- Choose the desired cells you wish to wrap, such as the range B2:B9.
- Access the drop-down menu for text wrapping and proceed to click on the Wrap option.

As a result, the cells will automatically adjust their size to accommodate the content within them.

1.12 Freezing Columns and Rows

When managing vast spreadsheets, there are moments when you yearn for the perpetual visibility of specific columns or rows, particularly when dealing with header cells. Thankfully, there is a solution that allows you to easily navigate through your spreadsheet while ensuring the header cells remain fixed. By freezing columns or rows, you can effortlessly view your data without losing sight of the crucial headers.

1.12.1 How to Freeze a Column

To ensure a seamless viewing experience when working with large spreadsheets, it's helpful to know how to freeze columns. Here's a step-by-step guide on how to do it:

- Identify the column you wish to freeze. Let's say you want to freeze the leftmost column. It's important to note that you don't need to select the columns you want to freeze.
- Look for the "View" option in the toolbar and click on it. A drop-down menu will appear.
- Hover your mouse over the "Freeze" option in the dropdown menu. You'll see a selection of different column freezing options.
- Choose the number of columns you want to freeze from the options provided.
- Voila! The leftmost column is now frozen in place. You can freely scroll through your worksheet without losing sight of the frozen column on the left.

1.12.2 Unfreezing a Column

To release columns from their fixed positions,

- Simply navigate to the View tab.
- Hover your cursor over the Freeze option.
- Proceed to choose the option to remove column freezing by clicking "No columns".

1.12.3 How to Freeze a Row

To freeze a row in place:

- Identify the specific row or rows you wish to keep fixed. For instance, let's say we want to keep the first two rows stationary. It's important to note that you don't have to highlight these rows beforehand.
- Locate the "View" option on the toolbar and give it a click.
- Next, hover your mouse over the "Freeze" function and choose the number of rows you wish to fix from the options presented in the dropdown menu.
- Voila! The selected rows are now securely affixed at the top, allowing you to effortlessly navigate through your spreadsheet while maintaining a constant view of those frozen rows.

1.12.4 Unfreezing a Row

To unfreeze rows,

- Navigate to the View tab and position your cursor over the Freeze option.

- From the drop-down menu, choose the option labeled "No rows".

1.13 Safeguarding Your Spreadsheet Against Accidental and Malicious Changes

In Google Sheets, the ability to effortlessly share and collaborate on spreadsheets has proven to be an invaluable asset. However, this convenience also brings forth the need for heightened vigilance in safeguarding your valuable data from unwarranted modifications.

Fortunately, there are three fundamental approaches to effectively addressing this concern. By implementing these strategies, users can ensure the integrity and security of their spreadsheet content, fostering a seamless and protected collaborative environment. Let's delve into these strategies to gain a better understanding of how to fortify your data against potential unauthorized alterations.

1.13.1 Protecting a Google Worksheet

Safeguard your Google Spreadsheet by protecting individual worksheets.

- This can be accomplished by navigating to the Tools menu and
- Selecting the Protect Sheet option.
- Similar to a Google Doc, you can establish permissions that grant editing rights to specific individuals: invited collaborators, yourself exclusively, or a designated group of collaborators.

If you wish to restrict collaborators from modifying particular cells, consider relocating those cells to a separate "Results" worksheet that is set to read-only. Remember, formulas can reference any worksheet, allowing you to grant access to data entry cells while securing formula-based cells within the protected worksheet.

1.13.2 Setting up Notifications

Stay in the loop with updates to your Google Spreadsheet by configuring notification rules.

- Simply navigate to the Tools menu, and
- Select Notification Rules.
- From there, you can customize your preferences to receive notifications for various changes. Whether it's modifications made to the entire spreadsheet, a specific worksheet, a particular cell or range of cells, collaborators involved, or form submissions, you can opt to receive instant notifications or a daily summary.

This way, you'll always be informed and up-to-date.

1.13.3 Setting Data Validation

When it comes to safeguarding your spreadsheets, the solutions above are a couple of simple options that can do the trick. These changes not only restrict editing access but also ensure that you receive notifications whenever any modifications have been made. However, if you find yourself in a situation where you need to protect specific cells or even just a single cell, Google Spreadsheets may not offer a straightforward solution. Thankfully, there's a workaround available: setting up data validation. This technique will enable you to achieve the desired level of protection for your valuable data.

Prevent modification of individual cells or a specific cell range by assigning mandatory values. You can select from text, number, list, or date options to define the required criteria. Each criterion offers additional configurations. For instance, a number cell can have a range or maximum value limitation; a text cell can be specified to include or exclude certain word(s); a date cell can be restricted to valid dates only; and a list cell can be limited to predefined options. An additional setting allows you to either alert the editor about unmet validation rules while permitting the change or forbid any alterations that fail to meet the criteria.

Data validation is an incredibly handy technique that prevents inadvertent modifications to cells containing formulas. Here's how you can implement it:

- To validate a specific cell or range, begin by selecting it.
- Next, opt for the text criteria and adjust the second dropdown to "equals."
- Proceed by inputting your desired cell formula into the empty box.
- Lastly, ensure that the Allow invalid data box remains unchecked.

1.14 Renaming a Spreadsheet

In their default state, sheets are assigned rather nondescript names like Sheet 1, Sheet 2, and so on. However, you have the freedom to assign them names that hold more significance.

To rename a sheet, follow these simple steps:

- Identify and click on the sheet tab that you wish to rename.
- Locate the down arrow situated on the sheet tab.
- Proceed by selecting the option titled "Rename."

1.15 Manually Importing a CSV File to Google Sheets

To import a CSV file into Google Sheets, follow these simple steps:

- Begin by navigating to the main menu of Google Sheets.
- Locate and click on the "Import" option.
- Next, either select your desired file or drag it directly into Google Sheets.
- From the drop-down menu, choose your preferred separator.

Google Sheets offers several separator options, including tabs, commas, or even custom symbols. If you're unsure which separator to use, don't worry. Google Sheets can automatically detect the most suitable option for you.

When importing CSV files, setting the appropriate separator is crucial. It instructs Google Sheets on how to organize your data into vertical columns, ensuring your information is well-structured. This step is essential for effectively filtering, aggregating, and analyzing your data.

- Afterward, simply select the Import Data button to import the file.

When using Google Sheets, you will be prompted to specify the import location. From there, you have several options at your disposal: appending, replacing, importing data only, or creating a fresh spreadsheet. And just like that, you're all set!

In addition to its core functionality, you have the option to transform your text into numbers, dates, or formulas. This feature proves particularly advantageous when dealing with unformatted data that requires conversion into numerical values for seamless data manipulation. By ensuring the accurate formatting of your numerical data, you gain the ability to extract, combine, and perform various mathematical operations on the values it contains. This versatility enables smoother data processing and analysis.

Chapter 2: Exploring Basic Functions and Formulas

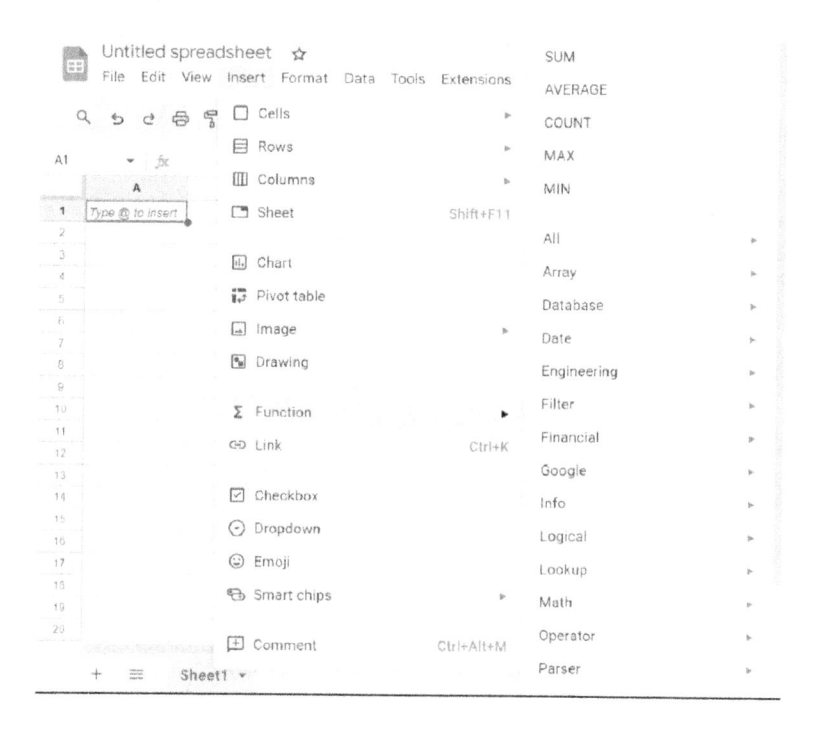

2.1 Understanding Functions

In spreadsheets, functions play a crucial role in simplifying complex calculations. They serve as predefined formulas used for performing computations with precision and efficiency. Google Sheets houses a plethora of these handy tools, allowing users to easily derive sums, averages, counts, maximums, and minimums for a given set of cells. To harness the power of functions, it is essential to be aware of their various parts and master the art of creating arguments that calculate both cell references and values.

2.2 The Parts of a Function

When it comes to inputting a function into a cell, the sequence matters. Syntax, the predetermined order of a function, must be adhered to for accurate calculation. To create a formula using a function, begin with an equal sign (=), followed by the function name (e.g., AVERAGE for finding an average), and an argument. Arguments comprise the data you wish the formula to process, like a range of cell references.

2.2.1 Arguments

In spreadsheets, arguments play a vital role, allowing for precise calculations and data manipulation. Whether it's a single cell or a range of cells, arguments are enclosed within parentheses, serving as the building blocks of powerful functions. The syntax varies depending on the desired outcome.

For instance, consider the function =AVERAGE(D1:D9), which simply computes the average of values within the cell range D1 to D9. Notice how this function consists of a single argument, encapsulating simplicity and clarity.

On the other hand, when dealing with multiple arguments, a comma serves as a separator. Take the function =SUM(B1:B3, E1:E2, G1), where the values from three distinct cell ranges are added together at once.

2.3 How to Create a Function

Google Sheets offers a wide range of functions to help you maximize your productivity. Let's take a look at a few essential functions that will undoubtedly become your go-to tools:

2.3.1 SUM

In Google Sheets, this function calculates the sum of all the cell values provided as an argument.

2.3.2 COUNT

The Count function is designed to tally the number of cells containing numerical data within the specified argument. It serves as a convenient tool for swiftly calculating the total of items within a range of cells.

2.3.3 AVERAGE

In this function, you can find the average of the values given as arguments. It works by adding up all the values and then dividing the sum by the total number of cells.

2.3.4 MIN

In this particular function, its purpose is to identify the minimum value found within the given argument.

2.3.5 MAX

In this function, the aim is to identify the maximum value among the cells provided within the argument.

2.3.6 Using the Functions Button to Create a Function

With the Functions button, you can easily generate results for a group of cells. The outcome will be shown in the cell located beneath the selected range.

Here's how you can make the most of this feature:

- Highlight the cells you wish to include in the equation by selecting them. Let's say we want E3:E12.
- Locate and click the Functions button, then choose the function that you want from the options that appear. In this case, let's go with SUM.
- The chosen function will be displayed in the cell directly below the selected cells.
- To calculate the function and view the result, simply press the Enter key on your keyboard.

2.3.7 Manually Creating a Function

If you're already familiar with the function name, there's a straightforward way to input it yourself.

Alright, let's dive in and explore a practical method for calculating numerical values in a range of cells. Specifically, we'll focus on entering different numerical values in cells B4 through B10. To derive the desired outcome, we'll employ the trusty AVERAGE function.

- Begin by selecting the cell where you want the result to appear, such as B11 in our case.

- Start the function by typing the equals sign (=), followed by the function name you desire. Alternatively, you can choose the function from the suggested list that pops up as you type. For instance, let's type =AVERAGE in our example.
- When manually inputting a function in Google Sheets, a window will appear listing the specific arguments required by the function. This window remains visible as you input the arguments, appearing once you type the first parenthesis.
- Inside the parentheses, enter the cell range for the argument. In our example, we'll type (B4:B10). This formula will sum the values in cells B4 to B10 and then divide that sum by the total number of values in that range.
- Finally, press the Enter key on your keyboard, and voila! The result will be displayed in the selected cell.

Quick Tip: In Google Sheets, it's important to be vigilant about checking your functions for errors, as the platform may not always alert you to them. Taking the time to review your functions is crucial.

2.4 Using the Function List

For those who are already proficient in working with spreadsheets and wish to leverage the capabilities of Google Sheets for more complex calculations, delving into the Google Sheets function list can prove to be incredibly useful. This comprehensive compilation serves as a valuable resource, offering a wide array of financial, statistical, and data analysis functions.

If you are well-versed in the functions available in Microsoft Excel's Function Library, you'll discover a striking similarity between the functions offered in Google Sheets' function list. This familiarity can facilitate a seamless transition and ensure a smooth experience when utilizing Google Sheets for your calculation needs.

2.4.1 Accessing the Function List in Google Sheet

To view the list of functions:

- Click on the Functions button and choose the option "More functions..." from the drop-down menu. This will open a new tab in your web browser.
- In the new tab, you will find a comprehensive list of functions available in Google Sheets.

2.5 Understanding the Basics of Google Sheets Formulas

Before diving deeper into everything there is to know about Google Sheets formulas, it's important to grasp the fundamental concepts. To construct a formula, you'll need logical expressions and functions, which are mathematical expressions with specific names. To let Google Sheets know that you're inputting a formula and not a regular number or text, simply begin with an equal sign (=) followed by the cell you want to work with. Then, enter the function name and complete the formula accordingly.

In your formula, you can include various components such as cell references, named data ranges, numeric and textual constants, operators, and additional functions. These elements work together to create a powerful and versatile formula that can handle complex calculations and data manipulation.

2.5.1 Cell References

There are three different types of cell references in Google Sheets. These references are essential for functions to access and manipulate data. To refer to a specific cell, a combination of letters for columns and numbers for rows is used. For instance, the first cell in column A is denoted as A1. By understanding these cell references, users can effectively work with data in Google Sheets.

In Google Sheets, cell references come in three distinct types:

2.5.1.1 Relative Cell Reference

The relative cell reference is represented by the format A1. This type allows the reference to adjust automatically as you copy or move it around.

2.5.1.2 Absolute Cell Reference

The absolute cell reference is denoted by the format $A$1. An absolute reference remains fixed regardless of any changes made to its position in the sheet.

2.5.1.3 Mixed Cell Reference

Combining aspects of relative and absolute references, the mixed format can be represented as $A1 or A$1. This type allows for flexibility in one direction while remaining fixed in the other.

By utilizing the dollar sign ($), you can determine and control the type of reference you wish to employ in your Google Sheets.

When you move a formula that contains relative cell references, those references adjust based on the new location. Let's say you have a formula in cell B1 that references cell A1. If you copy that formula to cell C2, the reference will change to B2. Since the formula was moved one column to the right and one row below, all the coordinates increased by 1.

On the other hand, formulas with absolute references remain unchanged when copied. They always point to the same cell, regardless of any new columns or rows added to the table or if the cell is moved elsewhere.

When you copy a formula from one cell to another, the references within the formula change accordingly. For example, if the original formula in cell B1 is "=A1," when you copy it to cell C2, it becomes "=B2." Similarly, if the original formula in B1 is "=A$1," when you copy it to C2, it becomes "=B$1." Likewise, if the original formula in B1 is "=$A1," when you copy it to C2, it becomes "=$A2." Lastly, if the original formula in B1 is "=$A$1," when you copy it to C2, it remains "=$A$1."

2.5.1.4 How to Prevent Cell References from Changing

To ensure that references remain constant even when copied or relocated, it is advisable to use absolute references.

2.5.1.5 Switching Between Relative, Absolute, and Mixed Cell References

To swiftly toggle between relative and absolute cell references, simply select the desired cell reference and hit the F4 key on your keyboard.

Initially, a relative reference like A1 will transform into an absolute reference, $A$1. Push the F4 key again, and you'll see a mixed reference, A$1. With another press of the button, you will see $A1. To revert everything back to its original state, press F4 once more.

Quick Tip: If you wish to change all references simultaneously, highlight the entire formula and press F4.

2.6 Data Ranges

In Google Sheets, you'll find more than just individual cell references. There's another handy feature called ranges, which allows you to refer to groups of adjacent cells. Ranges are defined by specifying the upper left and bottom right cells. So instead of just referencing a single cell like A1, you might encounter references like D1:E6, which encompass a range of cells. This flexibility in referencing makes it easier to work with multiple cells at once and perform operations on larger sets of data.

2.7 Constant Values

In Google Sheets, constant values are those that remain unchanged and cannot be calculated. These constants are typically represented by text or numbers, such as Income (text), 06/09/2023 (date), or 364 (number). While we cannot modify these values directly, we can manipulate them using the different operators and functions available.

Let's take a look at a couple of ways constants and formulas can be used in spreadsheets. Firstly, you can have a formula that consists of constant values and operators, like this: "=50+4*9". This formula performs the calculation and gives you the result.

On the other hand, formulas can also be used to calculate a new value by utilizing data from another cell. For instance, "=A5+700" adds 700 to the value in cell A5 and provides the updated result. With these simple examples, you can see how formulas and constants play a crucial role in performing calculations within spreadsheets.

2.7.1 Manually Changing Constant Values

At times, it becomes necessary to manually adjust the constants. The most straightforward approach is to assign each value to a distinct cell and use references in formulas. This way, modifications can be made in a single cell, saving you the hassle of altering multiple formulas.

For instance, if you input 700 in cell D3, you can refer to it in the formula:

=A5+D3

By merely changing the number in D3 to, let's say, 900, the result will be automatically recalculated accordingly.

H2 2.8 Working with Operators in Google Sheet Formulas Spreadsheets employ various operators to determine the type and sequence of calculations. These operators can be categorized into four distinct groups:

- Arithmetic Operators
- Comparison Operators
- Concatenation Operators
- Reference or Formula Operators

2.8.1 Arithmetic Operators

These operators, aptly named, are utilized for mathematical computations like addition, subtraction, multiplication, and division, ultimately yielding numerical results.

Arithmetic operators are fundamental tools in mathematical computation. Let's explore some of the commonly used operators and their operations.

- First, we have the plus sign (+), which signifies addition. For instance, "=3+3" would yield a sum of 6.
- Next, we encounter the minus sign (-), which denotes subtraction. For example, "=3-3" would result in zero.
- The same minus sign (-) can also be used to represent negative numbers. So, "=-3" indicates a negative value.
- Moving on, we have the asterisk (*), which signifies multiplication. If we evaluate "=3*3", the product would be 9.
- The slash (/) is the operator for division. For instance, "=3/3" would give us a quotient of 1.
- The percent sign (%) is used to calculate percentages. So, "30%" would represent half of a whole.
- Lastly, the caret sign (^) denotes exponents. For example, "=3^2" signifies raising 3 to the power of 2, resulting in 9.

2.8.2 Comparison Operators

When it comes to comparing values, comparison operators play a crucial role in determining whether the result is true or false. These operators evaluate two values and provide a logical expression as the outcome.

There are various ways to compare values in spreadsheets. Let's explore some of the comparison operators and their corresponding conditions.

- First, we have the "=" operator, which checks if two values are equal. For example, "=A1=B1" would evaluate whether the value in cell A1 is equal to the value in B1.
- Next, we have the ">" operator, which checks if one value is greater than another. For instance, "=A1>B1" would determine if the value in A1 is greater than the value in B1.
- Conversely, the "<" operator checks if a value is less than another. Using this operator, "=A1<B1" would ascertain if the value in A1 is less than the value in B1.
- Moving on, the ">=" operator checks if a value is greater than or equal to another. For example, "=A1>=B1" would check if the value in A1 is greater than or equal to the value in B1.
- Likewise, the "<=" operator checks if a value is less than or equal to another. So, "=A1<=B1" would verify if the value in A1 is less than or equal to the value in B1.
- Lastly, we have the "<>" operator, which checks if two values are not equal. Using this operator, "=A1<>B1" would determine if the value in A1 is not equal to the value in B1.

2.8.3 Concatenation Operators

The ampersand symbol (&) is a handy tool that allows you to merge different text strings together. In Google Sheets, you can use this symbol to combine words and create a cohesive phrase. For instance, if you type ="Air"&"craft" in a cell, it will display "Aircraft" as the result. Similarly, if you have a surname in cell A1 and a name in cell B1, you can combine them using the formula =A1&", "&B1 to obtain the full name in the format "Surname, Name."

2.8.4 Reference/Formula Operators

In Google Sheets, you can construct formulas and specify data ranges using reference or formula operators. These operators play a crucial role in formulating calculations within the spreadsheet application.

: (Colon)

Known as the Range Operator, this formula operator allows you to reference a range of cells from the first cell to the last cell that was mentioned. To use it, simply mention the first and last cells of the range. For instance, if you want to refer to cells A5 to A15, you would write them as A5:A15.

, (Comma)

Referred to as the Union Operator, this formula operator enables you to combine multiple references into a single reference. By using the comma, you can join multiple cell references together. For example, if you want to calculate the sum of cells A5 to A15 and C5 to C15, you would write it as =SUM(A5:A15,C5:C15).

2.9 Operator Precedence and Order of Calculations

In formula calculations, operators hold varying levels of importance. These priorities determine the order in which the calculations are performed and ultimately influence the resulting values.

In Google Sheets, each formula follows a specific pattern. Values are processed from left to right, taking into account the precedence of operators. When operators share the same level of priority, such as multiplication and division, they are evaluated in the order they appear, from left to right.

In a calculation, the operators have a specific order of precedence. Here's a simplified breakdown:

- Range Operators: These include the comma (,), space, and colon (:).
- Minus Sign: Represented by the symbol "-".
- Percentage: represented by the symbol "%".
- Exponentiation: Represented by the symbol "^".
- Multiplication and division are represented by the symbols "*" and "/".
- Addition and subtraction are represented by the symbols "+" and "-".
- Concatenation: Represented by the symbol "&" it is used to combine multiple textual strings into one.
- Comparison Operators: These include "=", "<>", "<=", or ">=", used for making comparisons.

2.9.1 Modifying the Order of Calculation with Brackets

To modify the order of calculations in a formula, simply use brackets to group the desired sections. Here's an example to demonstrate:

Consider the standard formula: =8+2*3. In this case, multiplication takes precedence, resulting in an answer of 14. However, by incorporating brackets, the equation takes on a new dynamic: =(8+2)*3. Now, the numbers within the brackets are added first, and the resulting sum is then multiplied by 3, yielding a value of 30.

In the given example, =(B3+30)/SUM(E3:E5), the brackets provide instructions for a series of calculations. First, it adds the value of B3 to 30. Then, it finds the sum of the values in cells E3, E4, and E5. Finally, it divides the first number from the result of B3+30 by the sum of the values in E3, E4, and E5.

Thankfully, these calculations should be familiar to us since we are accustomed to performing arithmetic operations in this order from a young age.

2.10 Named Ranges

Are you aware that you can assign labels to individual cells and data ranges in an entity? This simplifies the handling of extensive datasets and allows for faster navigation through Google Sheets formulas.

For instance, if you have a column that calculates the total revenue for each product and customer, you can label this range "Total_Revenue" and utilize it in your formulas. Undoubtedly, you'll find that the formula =SUM(Total_Revenue) is much more straightforward and readable compared to =SUM($A$3:$A$17).

Please note that it's not possible to create named ranges using non-adjacent cells.

2.10.1 Identifying Your Named Ranges

To identify your named range, follow these steps:

- Select your desired adjacent cells and make sure they are highlighted.
- Proceed to Data.
- In the sheet menu, select Named Ranges. This action will open a pane on the right side.
- Assign a name to the range and click on the "Done" button.

By doing this, you can easily manage and modify any ranges that you have created.

2.10.2 Naming Convention for Your Data Range

Google Sheets formulas become more user-friendly, transparent, and comprehensible when you employ named ranges. However, adhering to a few simple guidelines is crucial when it comes to assigning labels to these ranges.

When choosing a name for data ranges, there are a few guidelines to keep in mind.

- The name should consist of only underscores, numbers, or letters.
- It should not begin with a number or the words "true" or "false."
- Punctuation marks and spaces are not allowed.
- The length of the name should be between 1 and 250 characters.
- Lastly, it's important to avoid naming the range the same as the range itself, such as B2:C3, as this can lead to errors.

In case of an error, like using spaces in the name "Total Revenue," you will receive an immediate notification. It is important to use the correct naming convention, such as "TotalRevenue" or "Total_Revenue." It's worth noting that Google Sheets named ranges function similarly to absolute cell references. Regardless of adding or removing rows and columns within the table, the "Total_Revenue" range remains unaffected. You can freely move the range to different locations on the sheet without impacting the results.

2.11 Simple and Complex Formulas

Formulas come in various levels of complexity, from basic to intricate.

2.11.1 Basic Google Sheet Formulas

Constants, references to cells on the same page, and operators are all parts of simple formulas. In general, there is only one function or operator involved, and the calculations are performed in the following order, from left to right:

=SUM(B3:B14)

=B1+C1

2.11.2 Complex Google Sheet Formulas

When additional functions and operators come into play or the order of calculations becomes more intricate, formulas can quickly become complex. These complex formulas often involve cell references, multiple functions, constants, operators, and named ranges, making them lengthy and overwhelming. Deciphering them can be a challenge, and typically only the author can do so, especially if the formula was created recently.

2.11.3 Tips for Reading Complex Formulas Without Stress

This is a clever technique to enhance the readability of your formulas. By employing an ample number of spaces and line breaks, you can easily organize your formulas in a visually coherent manner without compromising their functionality.

- To insert a line break within a formula, simply use Alt+Enter on your keyboard.
- For a complete view of the entire formula, expand the Formula bar.

Without the inclusion of these additional spaces and line breaks, the formula would appear convoluted, like in the following example:

=ArrayFormula(MAX(IF(($D$3:$D$14=A19)*($B$3:$B$14=E20), $A$1:$A$9,"")))

Clearly, opting for the former approach significantly improves the formula's legibility and ease of comprehension.

2.12 Using Logical Functions

Unlock the power of logical functions in Google Sheets, such as NOT, AND, OR, and more. Discover how to seamlessly integrate them with the IF function and comparison operators.

Logical operators play a crucial role in computer decision-making, enabling even the most basic tasks like sorting orders by geographical region. Without these operators, the process would be a hassle.

2.12.1 OR(), AND(), and NOT() Functions

In logical operations, various conditions are put to the test, and depending on their fulfillment or non-fulfillment, specific events are triggered. Three fundamental logical operators exist: the NOT operator, the OR operator, and the AND operator. When working with Google Sheets, these operators manifest themselves as the NOT(), OR(), and AND() functions, respectively. Through the utilization of these functions, the fulfillment or non-fulfillment of conditions can be effectively evaluated.

- Similar to the NOT logical operator, the NOT() function reverses the value from true to false or vice versa.
- When utilizing the AND() function, it assesses two cells to determine if both are true. If they are, the output is true; otherwise, it is false.
- The OR() function produces a TRUE value when at least one of the referenced cells contains TRUE. If both cells hold FALSE, the output is FALSE.
- While the NOT() function solely relies on a single cell as a reference, both the OR() and AND() functions can handle input from multiple cells. The same principles apply:
a) If any of the cells in the reference array contain false, the AND() function will yield a false value.
b) Conversely, if any of the cells in the reference array contain true, the OR() function will produce a true value.

2.12.2 Using Comparison Operators with Logical Functions

In order to deepen our understanding of the potency of logical functions, let's explore their integration with comparison operators. These operators serve the purpose of comparing two values and determining whether a specific condition is met. Among the comparison operators at our disposal are the equals operator, the greater than operator, and the less than operator.

When we include comparison operators in our formulas, they generate a true or false result. This functionality makes them a perfect match for logical functions. If we need to compare two numbers from separate cells, we can easily do so by following this format:

=<cell1><comparison_operator_to_use><cell2></cell2></comparison_operator_to_use></cell1>

Alternatively, we can use comparison functions in a similar way:

=<cell1><comparison_operator_to_use><cell2></cell2></comparison_operator_to_use></cell1>

Chapter 3: Spreadsheet Customization and Formatting

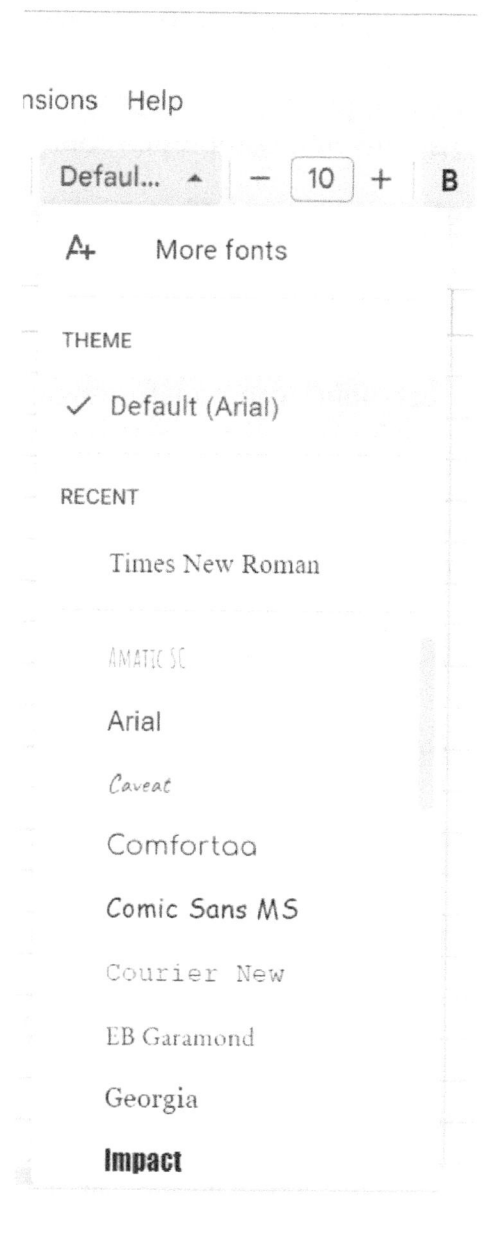

nsions Help

Defaul... ▲ — 10 + B

A+ More fonts

THEME

✓ Default (Arial)

RECENT

Times New Roman

AMATIC SC

Arial

Caveat

Comfortaa

Comic Sans MS

Courier New

EB Garamond

Georgia

Impact

3.1 Formatting Cells

When your spreadsheet is filled with a substantial amount of data, it can become challenging to navigate and comprehend all the information at a glance. Fortunately, formatting comes to the rescue, empowering you to personalize the appearance of your spreadsheet for enhanced visibility and comprehension.

In this chapter, we will delve into the art of modifying text attributes within cells. From adjusting the size, style, and color of your text to aligning it precisely and incorporating borders and background colors, we will explore how these formatting techniques can transform your spreadsheet into a visually appealing and easily readable masterpiece.

In a fresh spreadsheet, all cells share a common default format. However, you have the freedom to tailor the formatting to enhance the clarity and comprehension of your data.

3.1.1 Modifying the Font

Opting for a distinct font can effectively delineate specific sections of your spreadsheet, such as the header cells, from the remaining data. This can enhance visual clarity and make it easier to navigate through your information.

- Choose the cell or cells you wish to alter.
- Find and click on the Format option in the toolbar menu.
- Place your cursor over the Font tab and pick a different font from the provided options. Let's go with Georgia in this instance.

- Observe as the text transforms into the newly selected font.

3.1.2 Modifying the Font Size

Adjusting the size of the font can be a useful technique to emphasize significant cells and enhance readability. In this case, we can choose to enlarge the header cells in order to differentiate them from the other cells in the spreadsheet. By doing so, it becomes easier to identify and focus on these specific cells.

- First, you need to choose the cell or cells that you wish to make changes to.
- Look for the Font Size button on the toolbar and click on it. A drop-down menu will appear, allowing you to select the desired font size. For the header demonstration above, let's go with 14 to increase the text size.
- Once you've made your selection, the text will automatically adjust to the new font size.

3.1.3 Adding Underline and Italics to Your Text

- Highlight the text you wish to modify.
- Use the keyboard shortcut Command+U for Mac or Ctrl+U for Windows to underline. Push Command+I on Mac or Ctrl+I on Windows to add italics to your text.

3.1.4 Making Your Text Bold

When you want to emphasize your text, there's a simple way to make it bold. Just follow these steps:

- Highlight the text you wish to modify.
- To give it a bold appearance, either click the Bold text button or use the keyboard shortcut Command+B for Mac or Ctrl+B for Windows.
- You'll notice the text instantly transforms into a bolder, more prominent style.

3.1.5 Changing the Text Color

- Choose the specific cell or cells that require adjustment.
- Navigate to the toolbar and locate the Text Color button.
- Once found, click on it, and a drop-down menu showcasing an array of text colors will be revealed.
- Carefully opt for the desired color you wish to apply. For illustrative purposes, let's go with the color red.
- Witness the transformative effect as the text transitions to its vibrant new color.

3.2 Working with Text Alignment

In your spreadsheet, the default alignment positions any text you enter to the bottom-left of a cell, while numbers are aligned to the bottom-right. However, you have the flexibility to modify the alignment of your cell content and decide where it will be displayed.

3.2.1 Vertical Text Alignment

To adjust the vertical alignment of your text, follow these steps:

- Highlight the text you wish to adjust.
- Locate and click the vertical align button on the toolbar.
- From the options presented in the drop-down menu, select the desired alignment.
- Watch as your text easily adjusts to the new alignment.

3.2.2 Horizontal Text Alignment

To adjust the horizontal alignment of your text, follow these steps:

- Highlight the text that needs modification.
- Locate and click on the horizontal alignment button found in the toolbar. A drop-down menu will appear.
- Choose the desired alignment option from the menu.
- Your text will instantly adjust to the selected alignment.

3.3 Customizing Cell Borders and Fill (Background) Colors

When it comes to organizing your spreadsheet, background colors and cell borders play a crucial role in establishing distinct and well-defined boundaries for each section. These visual elements enable you to easily demarcate different areas, ensuring clarity and ease of comprehension.

3.3.1 How to Change the Fill Color

Altering the background color of a cell, commonly referred to as the fill color, is a straightforward process.

- Begin by selecting the desired cell or cells for modification.
- Locate the toolbar and click on the Fill Color button.
- Click on the button to reveal a drop-down menu of color options. For this demonstration, we will opt for the color green.
- Once selected, the new fill color will promptly manifest in the designated cell(s).

3.3.2 How to Add Cell Borders

To enhance the appearance of your cells by adding borders, follow these steps:

- Begin by selecting the cell or cells you wish to adjust.
- Locate and click on the Borders button, which will reveal a drop-down menu containing various border options. For instance, if you want to display borders around all the cells, make that selection.

- Once you've made your choice, the selected cells will showcase the newly added borders, giving them a refined and polished look.

3.4 Conditional Formatting Rules

In spreadsheets, you have the power to transform the appearance of your cells, rows, or columns based on specific criteria. By setting conditions, such as the presence of a particular word or number, you can change how your data is shown by altering the text or background colors.

- To begin, open Google Sheets on your computer.
- Next, select the specific cells that you wish to apply format rules to.
- Locate the "Format" option in the menu and click on it. From the dropdown menu, click on "Conditional formatting." This action will open a convenient toolbar on the right side of your screen.
- Now, it's time to create your format rule. There are two options available:
a) Single color: Under the "Format cells if" section, pick the condition that will set off the rule. Then, in the "Formatting Style," select the appearance you want the cell to have when the conditions are met.
b) Color scale: In the "Preview" section, you can pick a color scale that suits your needs. Additionally, determine a minimum and maximum value, and if you like, a midpoint value. To specify the value category, click on the downward arrow.
- Once you're satisfied with your format rule, click "Done" to finalize and apply it.

In this example, an educator can easily identify students who scored below 70% on a test using Google Sheets. Here's how:

- Launch a spreadsheet in Google Sheets on your computer.
- Highlight the test scores you want to analyze.
- Go to the "Format" menu and select "Conditional formatting."
- Choose the option "less than" in the "Format cells if" section. If there's already a rule, either select it or add a new one, and then choose "Less than."
- Click on "Value or formula" and enter 0.7.
- To highlight the low scores in red, select "Fill."
- Click "Done," and you'll see the scores below 70% highlighted in red.

3.5 Making and Formatting a Google Sheet Table

When working with data in Google Sheets, you often start with a collection of dates, numbers, or ordinary text values. But have you ever considered the benefits of organizing this data into a structured table? By doing so, you can greatly improve your ability to analyze and present information in a more efficient and meaningful way.

Tables play a crucial role in organizing and connecting data within a spreadsheet. While the concept of tables is universal, the specific features and functionality can vary across different spreadsheet software. If you're accustomed to using Excel tables, you might not be aware of the unique capabilities offered by Google Sheets' tables. But in spite of that, these features are not missing; they simply operate in a different way.

In this section, we'll explore the process of creating a basic table in Google Sheets. Once you've established a foundational table structure, we'll delve into formatting techniques that will make it easily recognizable as a table. Additionally, we'll learn methods to improve the functionality of your table, such as enabling filtering, collapsing, and searchability.

3.5.1 Creating Your First Google Sheets Table

Let's begin by understanding the process of creating a basic table in Google Sheets.

- Start by navigating to Google Sheets and opening a new sheet.
- Next, include column headers to label the different categories of data.
- Finally, input the relevant row data to populate the table with information.

And there you have it! A basic table in Google Sheets is now at your fingertips. In the upcoming sections, we'll delve into the art of refining this table, transforming it into an aesthetically pleasing, easily searchable, and organized masterpiece.

3.5.2 Formatting Your Google Sheets Table

With your basic table in place, it's time to jazz things up a bit by tweaking the formatting and enhancing its features.

By making a few adjustments, you can transform the look and functionality of your table. So let's dive in and explore how you can give your table a personal touch and make it more dynamic. Get ready to take your table to the next level!

3.5.3 The Application of Alternating Row Colors

- Begin by selecting the range of cells that make up your table, including the headers.
- To give your table a visually appealing touch, navigate to the Format menu and choose the option for alternating colors.
- Google Sheets is designed to intelligently identify the headers and will automatically mark them as such. However, if it fails to do so, you can manually check the "Header" box.
- Google Sheets offers a selection of predefined styles to choose from, or you can unleash your creativity by customizing the colors for the header and the alternating rows.
- Take a moment to look at your handiwork, and once you're satisfied with the appearance of your table, simply click "Done". If you ever wish to remove the alternating colors, just click the prominently placed red button.

3.5.4 Making a Filtered Table

It's worth mentioning that in Google Sheets, you can only have one filtered table per sheet. To work with multiple filtered tables in a single file, ensure that each one is placed on a separate sheet or tab. To enable filters for each column, follow the steps below. This will allow you to easily filter and sort your data with just a few clicks.

To format tables in Google Sheets, the process is surprisingly straightforward.

- First, choose any of the headers in your table.
- Then, navigate to the "Data" menu and select "Create a filter."
- Now, you'll notice that a filter icon appears next to each header.
- To sort and filter your data, simply click on the filter icon in any column. This will display the available options for sorting and filtering your table.

3.5.5 Making Your Table Collapsible

When working with a sizable table, it can be helpful to condense the columns or rows for easier viewing. Although one option is to hide specific columns or rows, this approach can be prone to errors. A more efficient alternative is to group the columns or rows, allowing for collapsible sections in your table.

3.5.6 How to Group Table Columns

Here's a simplified guide to help you organize and categorize table columns for convenient collapsing and expanding.

- Choose the specific columns you intend to collapse.
- Access the menu by right-clicking in the section where the column letters are located, then clicking

on "View additional column actions." From there, opt to organize the columns into groups by clicking on the given option.
- Simply click on the minus icon situated above the first grouped column.
- And voila! To expand the columns, just click on the plus icon.

3.5.7 Grouping Table Rows

To organize the rows in your table, follow these simple steps:

- Highlight all the rows, excluding the headers.
- Access the menu by right-clicking on the row number area and choosing "View more row actions". From there, select the option to group the rows.
- To collapse the rows, click on the minus icon located in the upper-left area.
- That's all there is to it. To expand the table once again, just click on the plus icon in the upper-left area.

3.5.8 Creating a Searchable Table in Google Sheets

When it comes to working with data in formulas or tables, named ranges can be a real time saver. By assigning names to particular columns or specific ranges, you can easily reference and manipulate data. This eliminates the need to search through lengthy tables or formulas, making your workflow more efficient.

In this section, I'll walk you through the steps to name your entire table and its columns and provide examples of how to use named ranges with Google Sheets functions.

3.5.8.1 Giving Your Table a Name

- Begin by selecting the range of cells that make up your table.
- Navigate to the "Data" tab and click on "Named Ranges.".
- Enter a desired name for your table and click "Done".
- Your table will now be visible in the sidebar under "Named Ranges.".

3.5.8.2 Assigning a Name to a Specific Column to Make It Searchable

- To assign a name to a specific column within the table, simply select the column.
- Click on "Add a range".
- Once the column has been named, you can refer to it in other cells.

3.5.8.3 A Working Example of Searching with Columns

Let's take a practical scenario: calculating the total sum of purchases.

- Begin by typing the SUM function in an empty cell.
- Then, after the parenthesis, begin to type the column name. A suggestion box will emerge, offering options.
- Simply click on the desired column or hit the Tab key to select it.
- After closing the parenthesis, hit Enter, and voila! You now have the sum of all your purchases right there. It's as simple as that.

3.6 Making and Formatting Charts and Graphs

3.6.1 Making a Chart or Graph

To create a chart or graph

- Launch Google Sheets on your computer and access a spreadsheet.
- Highlight the cells that you wish to incorporate into your chart.
- Navigate to the Insert tab and select Chart to begin the process.

3.6.2 How to Switch the Type of Chart

If you intend to give your data visuals a different look, you can easily change the chart type in Google Sheets. Follow these simple steps to personalize your charts:

- Begin by opening the desired spreadsheet in Google Sheets on your computer.

- Locate the chart you wish to modify and give it a double-click.
- On the right-hand side, find and click on the "Setup" option.
- Look for the "Chart type" section and click on the downward arrow symbol.
- A list of chart options will appear. Select the desired chart type from the available choices.

3.6.3 Changing the Data Range

Changing the data range in Google Sheets is a straightforward process. Here's how you can do it:

- Start by opening the spreadsheet in Google Sheets on your computer.
- Locate the chart that you wish to modify and double-click on it.
- On the right-hand side, you'll find the Setup option. Click on it.
- Look for the "Data Range" section and click on the Grid option below it.
- Now, you can select the specific cells that you want to include in your chart.
- If you need to incorporate additional data into the chart, click on the Add another range button. Then, choose the desired cells to add.
- Once you're done, simply click OK to finalize the changes.

3.6.4 Adding Gridlines

Incorporating gridlines into various types of charts can significantly enhance data readability. Whether you're working with candlestick, radar, histogram, waterfall, scatter, bar, column, area, or line charts, gridlines serve as a valuable tool. To customize your chart's gridlines in Google Sheets, follow these steps:

- Launch Google Sheets on your computer and open the desired spreadsheet.
- Double-click on the chart you intend to modify.
- On the right-hand side, locate and click on the "Customize" option.
- Look for the "Gridlines" section and select it.
- If your chart displays both vertical and horizontal gridlines, you can specify which gridlines to alter by choosing the appropriate option beside "Apply to."
- Proceed to make the desired adjustments to the gridlines according to your preferences.

3.6.4.1 Tips and Tricks for Gridlines

The following are quick tips and tricks to personalize your gridlines:

- For personalized gridline numbers, simply input your desired number in the designated box labeled "Minor gridline count" or "Major gridline count."
- If you want to conceal gridlines while retaining axis labels, opt for matching colors for both the gridlines and chart background.

3.6.5 Customizing Points and Bars on a Chart

You can edit individual points and bars on your charts to customize them to your taste. Follow these steps to easily improve your chart:

- Begin by opening a spreadsheet in Google Sheets on your computer.
- Locate the chart and right-click on the desired bar or point.
- A menu will appear; click on "Format Data Point."
- Now, you can make any desired changes to the selected point or bar.

Remember, while you can add borders to bars and columns, this option is not available for points or lines.

3.6.6 Changing Your Chart's Font, Background, and Other Features

You have the option to change your chart's font, background, and some other features. However, the options available for modification will vary depending on the specific type of chart you are working with. Here's a step-by-step guide to help you make these adjustments:

- Begin by opening a spreadsheet in Google Sheets on your computer.
- Locate and double-click on the chart that you wish to modify.
- On the right-hand side of the screen, you'll find the "Customize" option. Click on it.
- Next, select "Chart style" from the available menu.

- Now, you can proceed to implement the desired modifications to the chart, making it more tailored to the changes you want.

3.6.7 Customizing Chart Titles, Subtitles, and Their Fonts

When working with charts, you have the option to add titles and subtitles to various chart types, such as treemap, candlestick, radar, histogram, waterfall, pie, scatter, bar, column, area, and line charts.

To make changes to your titles, subtitles, or fonts, follow these simple steps:

- Access Google Sheets on your computer and open the desired spreadsheet.
- Double-click on the chart that requires modification.
- On the right side of the screen, locate and click on the "Customize" option.
- Look for the "Chart & Axis Title" section and click on it.
- Select the specific title you intend to modify next to "Type."
- Input the desired title text in the designated "Title text" field.
- Feel free to make further adjustments to the title and font as needed.

Remember, for any existing titles on the chart that require editing, simply double-click on them to begin the changes.

3.6.8 Customizing Chart Legends, such as Color, Style, Font, or Position

A chart legend serves as a guide, describing the data in the chart. It can be added to various types of charts, including radar, histogram, waterfall, pie, scatter, bar, column, area, and line charts.

To modify a chart's legend in Google Sheets, follow these steps:

- Open a spreadsheet in Google Sheets on your computer.
- Locate the desired chart and double-click on it.
- On the right-hand side, click on the "Customize" option, then select "Legend."
- From there, you can personalize your legend by adjusting its color, style, font, or position.

Note: For individual changes to specific legend items, simply double-click on the respective text.

3.6.8.1 Adding or Editing the Legend Header

To modify or update the legend header in your Google Sheets spreadsheet, follow these steps:

- Begin by opening the desired spreadsheet on your computer using Google Sheets.
- Locate and double-click the chart that requires modification.

- Note: Ensure that the text you wish to display in the legend is positioned in the first column or row of your data set.
- On the right side of the screen, find and click on the "Setup" option.
- Next, you will need to choose an appropriate action based on your specific situation.
a) If your headers are arranged in rows, select the "Use row N as headers" option.
b) If your headers are arranged in columns, select the "Switch rows/columns" option, followed by choosing "Use column N as headers."

Quick Tip: If you wish to customize a singular legend item, simply double-click on the corresponding text.

3.6.9 Working with Chart Items

You hold the power to manipulate, adjust, or remove various elements from your charts at your will. Whether it's shifting their position, altering their size, or completely eliminating them, you have the freedom to mold your chart into whatever form you desire.

3.6.9.1 Removing Items from Your Chart

There are times when you may want to tidy up your chart by removing certain elements such as error bars, data labels, legends, and titles. Deleting these items is an easy process.

3.6.9.2 Deleting Specific Items

- If you wish to remove a particular item on the chart, simply double-click on it and then press the backspace or delete key.

3.6.9.3 Deleting Error Bars or Data Labels

- To delete error bars or data labels, start by double-clicking on any one of them to select all.
- Then, click a third time to choose the individual data label or bar you want to delete.

3.6.9.4 Removing Other Items

Remember, if you want to remove other items from your chart, just double-click on the chart itself to access the side panel and make the necessary adjustments.

3.6.9.5 Moving Items on Your Chart

When working with charts, you can rearrange chart elements such as labels, titles, and legends. Though certain elements, like pie chart labels and data-showing parts of a chart, defy relocation, others can be effortlessly shifted. Here's how:

- To relocate an item to a new spot, simply double-click on the desired item within the chart.
- Next, drag the item to its intended location.

- Alternatively, you can utilize the arrow keys on your keyboard to relocate the desired item.

3.6.9.6 Resetting the Location of an Item

- To restore the position of a singular item, right-click on it and select "Reset layout."

3.6.9.7 Resetting the Location of All Items

- If you intend to reset the positioning of all items, double-click on the chart itself to launch the chart editor.
- Navigate to the "Customize" tab and click on Chart Style Reset Layout.

3.6.10 Moving a Chart

To relocate a chart in Google Sheets, take the following actions:

- Begin by opening a spreadsheet on your computer using Google Sheets.
- Identify the chart that needs to be moved and select it with a click.
- Drag the chart to the desired location within the spreadsheet.

For those looking to move multiple items simultaneously, hold down the Command key on Mac or the CTRL key on

Windows while clicking on the respective items to be moved.

3.6.11 Resizing a Chart

To adjust the dimensions of a chart in Google Sheets, follow these steps:

- Access Google Sheets on your computer and open the desired spreadsheet.
- Locate and select the chart that you wish to modify.
- To resize the chart, simply click and drag the blue markers.

Quick Tip: If you want to resize multiple items simultaneously, hold down the CTRL on Windows (or Command for Mac) key while clicking on the items you want to adjust.

3.6.12 Quickly Navigating Your Charts with Keyboard Shortcuts

Navigating a chart is made easy when you choose to use the available keyboard shortcuts.

- Switch easily between chart elements by using the Tab key.
- Quickly cycle through the element layers by pressing the Enter key to select different parts of the chart.
- Use the Tab key to explore various objects at the selected level.
- Use Shift and Tab to move backward through the objects.

- Use the Esc key to jump out of a level.
- Hit the Enter key to dive into another level.

Chapter 4: Data Management

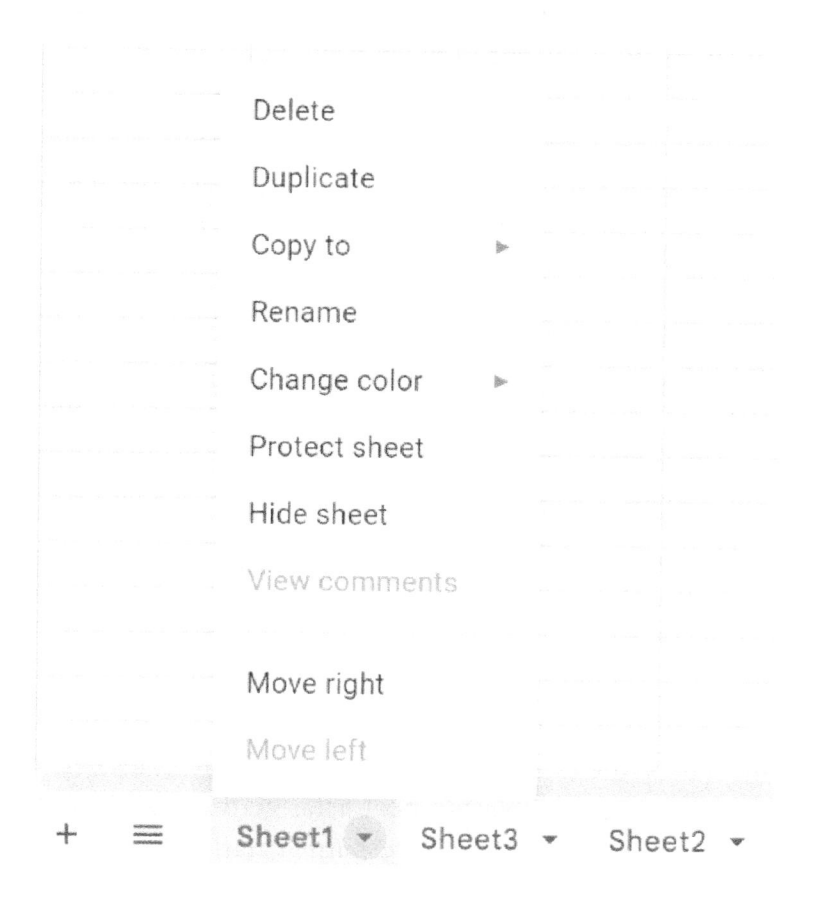

Delete

Duplicate

Copy to ▶

Rename

Change color ▶

Protect sheet

Hide sheet

View comments

Move right

Move left

\+   ≡   Sheet1 ▾   Sheet3 ▾   Sheet2 ▾

4.1 Sorting and Filtering Data

Google Sheets provides a powerful tool for managing and analyzing large amounts of data. As your spreadsheet grows with additional content, it becomes increasingly crucial to effectively organize the information within it. Google Sheets offers the capability to restructure your data by employing sorting and filtering functions.

Sorting enables you to arrange your data numerically or alphabetically, facilitating a clearer view and improved organization. On the other hand, filtering allows you to narrow down the data displayed, selectively revealing only the information that is relevant to your needs.

In this section, you'll discover how to utilize these features to enhance your spreadsheet management and improve your data analysis process.

4.1.1 Types of Sorting

When it comes to organizing data effectively, it's crucial to determine whether you want the sorting to be applied to a particular selection of cells or the whole sheet.

- Sorting the entire sheet allows you to arrange all the data in your spreadsheet based on one column. This ensures that related information across each row remains together once the sort is applied. Let's take the example of a client name list. By sorting the Name column in alphabetical order, the client names are displayed in a neat arrangement, with their corresponding address information maintained alongside.

- On the other hand, sorting a range of cells is useful when dealing with a sheet that contains multiple tables. This enables you to sort the data within a particular range without affecting other content on the worksheet.

4.1.2 Sorting a Range

To sort a particular range of data in a particular order, let's say you have a secondary table in a textbook order form and you want to organize the number of books ordered by class. Here's how you can do it:

- Start by selecting the range of cells that you wish to sort. For instance, let's assume you have entered data in the range A4:B7. Simply highlight this range by clicking and dragging the cursor over it.
- Next, navigate to the "Data" tab and click on it. A drop-down menu will appear, and from there, choose the option "Sort range."
- As you do this, you'll be presented with a sorting dialog box. Within this dialog box, you can select the specific column that you want to sort the data by. In your case, choose the appropriate column that corresponds to the class.
- After selecting the desired column, you can specify whether you want the sorting to be in ascending or descending order. To illustrate, let's assume you want to sort the data in descending order (from Z to A). Simply make this selection.
- Finally, click on the "Sort" button to start the sorting process. Once completed, the range of data will be organized according to your chosen criteria. In this example, the data will be sorted in descending order based on the Orders column.

4.1.3 Sorting a Sheet

In order to sort a spreadsheet, let's take the example of sorting a list of customers in alphabetical order based on their last names. To ensure accurate sorting, make sure your worksheet has a header row that identifies each column. To prevent the header labels from being included in the sort, we will freeze the header row.

Here's how you can do it:

- Go to the "View" tab and position your mouse over the "Freeze" option. From the menu that appears, select "1 row."
- The header row will now be frozen. Next, decide which column you want to sort and click on any cell within that column.
- Proceed to the "Data" tab and choose either "Sort Sheet by Column, A-Z (ascending)" or "Sort Sheet by Column, Z-A (descending)." For our example, let's select "Sort Sheet by Column, A-Z."
- The sheet will be sorted according to your selection, with the customers' last names organized alphabetically.

4.2 Creating a Filter

To apply a filter to a worksheet and display specific items, such as shovels and lawn mowers, follow these steps:

- First, ensure your worksheet has a header row to identify column names. Freeze the header row to prevent it from being included in the filter.

- Go to View and position your mouse over the "Freeze" option. Choose "1 row" to freeze the header row from the menu that is displayed.
- Click on any cell that has data.
- Select the filter button.
- In every column header, a drop-down arrow will be displayed.
- Go to the column you would like to filter and click on the corresponding dropdown arrow, such as column B for Tools in our example.
- Select "Clear" to get rid of every check.
- Choose the data you would like to filter, and then hit the OK button. For instance, check shovels and lawn mowers to view only these types of tools.
- You will find the filtered data, and every other piece of content that does not correspond to your filter criteria will be hidden. In this instance, only shovels and lawn mowers will be visible.

4.2.1 How to Apply More Than One Filter

Applying multiple filters can help you narrow down your search results effectively. Let's say you've already filtered your worksheet to display shovels and lawn mowers, but now you want to further refine it to show only the ones checked out in October.

To do this:

- Go to the column you wish to filter and click on the corresponding drop-down arrow. For instance, we'll add a filter to column D to sort the information by date.
- Choose the checkboxes that correspond to the data you want to filter, and then hit the OK button. In our case, we'll uncheck everything except for October.
- You will find the new filter applied to the result, resulting in a filtered worksheet that displays only lawn mowers and shovels checked out in October.

4.2.2 Creating a Filter View During Collaboration

When working together on a sheet, it's convenient to create a filter view. This feature lets you filter data without impacting how others see it—only your view is affected. Additionally, filter views allow you to name and save multiple views.

- To create a filter view, simply proceed to the Filter button and click on the dropdown arrow next to it.

4.2.3 Clearing Every Applied Filter

To remove any applied filters and restore the spreadsheet to its initial view, follow these steps:

- Locate and select the Filter button.
- Upon clicking the Filter button, all active filters will be deactivated, and the spreadsheet will revert to its original state. This action effectively eliminates any filtering criteria that may have been previously applied.

4.3 Data Validation

Ensuring accurate data types in your Google Sheets is crucial, particularly for shared spreadsheets where you want to avoid accidental tampering with data inputs. That's why data validation is a must. In this section, we'll delve into data validation, exploring its significance and how it can help maintain the integrity of your spreadsheets.

4.3.1 What is Data Validation?

Data validation in Google Sheets is a powerful tool for controlling the input type and range of data added to a spreadsheet. By adding data validation to the sheets, you can ensure that users receive error messages or have their input rejected if it falls outside the specified data range or doesn't match the required cell data.

4.3.2 Using Data Validation

Let's take a look at a couple of instances where the data validation feature in Google Sheets proves its worth:

4.3.2.1 Using Data Validation to Create a Dropdown List

In this scenario, you can conveniently record the birth month of different students in a single column. Since there are only twelve months to choose from, you can utilize the data validation feature in Google Sheets to create a dropdown menu. Here's how you can do it:

- Begin by selecting the cells where you want to implement the data validation.
- Once the cells are selected, navigate to the top bar and click on "Data," then select "Data Validation."
- In your spreadsheet, you should have a range of cells containing the months of the year. Note: It's also possible to store the data for the dropdown menu in a separate sheet and perform data validation from there.
- Choose the "Dropdown (from a range)" option under "Criteria" to include the months in the dropdown list.
- After adding the cell range to the dropdown list, click the green "Done" button to save your changes.

Now, you will notice a pill-shaped symbol in the cell, which allows you to reach the dropdown list. Simply click on the pill-shaped symbol to display the menu, where you'll find the specified parameters, such as January to December.

4.3.2.2 Using Data Validation to Set a Number Limit

Let's take this scenario: we encounter a dataset comprising the names of nine students and a space for inputting their scores on a test. It's crucial to ensure that the scores fall within the range of 0 to 100. Let's explore how you can employ the data validation feature in Google Sheets to accomplish this:

- Begin by selecting the cells where you want to implement data validation by clicking and dragging your cursor across them.
- Once the cells are selected, navigate to the top bar and click on "Data," then choose "Data Validation." This action will reveal the Data Validation Rules menu on the right side of the screen.
- Confirm that the "Apply to range" textbox encompasses the desired cell range for data validation.
- Next, click on the "Criteria" option, and from the dropdown menu, select "Is between."
- Two textboxes will appear beneath the "Criteria" option, enabling you to establish the minimum and maximum values. In this instance, we will use 0 and 100 as the respective values.
- Towards the end of the window, you have the option to determine the course of action when invalid data is entered. In our case, we can opt to display a warning.
- Finally, click on the "Done" button in green to save the modifications.

Henceforth, any values entered between 0 and 100 will be accepted by Google Sheets without triggering an error. However, if a value below 0 or above 100 is entered, Google Sheets will show an error indicator in the form of a small red triangle positioned at the upper right area of the cell. By hovering over the triangle, you can view the complete error explanation.

4.3.2.3 Using Data Validation to Check Dates

In Google Sheets, you have the option to verify dates using data validation. This feature allows you to determine whether a date falls before, after, or on the same day as a particular reference date. For instance, let's say you want to identify students who submitted their assignments late based on the submission date.

Here's a step-by-step guide on how to utilize this functionality:

- Begin by selecting the cells where you want to implement data validation.
- Once the desired cells are highlighted, navigate to the top bar and click on "Data," then select "Data Validation."
- Within the "Criteria" section, opt for the "Date is on or before" option. A text box will appear, enabling you to choose the reference date (yesterday, tomorrow, or the current date).
- Since you may intend to specify a specific date, you can utilize the DATE formula to input the desired date.
- Finally, click on the green "Done" button to save your changes.

Upon executing the formula, the dates exceeding the specified reference date will be highlighted. Hovering your cursor over these dates will display a pop-up message explaining the reason for the data validation failure.

4.3.2.4 Using Data Validation with a Custom Formula

Using a custom formula in conjunction with data validation opens up a world of possibilities for achieving specific outcomes. Unlike the predefined options in the data validation menu, custom formulas allow you to establish precise criteria tailored to your needs. To illustrate, let's consider the use of the LEN formula to ensure that cell contents do not exceed six characters.

To implement a custom formula in Google Sheets data validation, follow these steps:

- Select the desired cells by clicking and dragging over them.
- Once the cells are selected, navigate to the top bar and click on "Data," then select "Data Validation."
- Choose the "Custom Formula is" option under Criteria in the Data Validation Rules menu.
- You will see a new textbox, allowing you to input the desired formula.
- Enter your formula in the displayed text box, specifying the criteria you want to apply.
- Finally, save your changes by clicking the green "Done" button.

Upon executing the formula, any cells containing more than six characters will be visually highlighted, drawing attention to potential discrepancies.

4.4 Managing and Organizing Your Sheets and Tabs

To begin, it's crucial to understand that a Google Spreadsheet functions as a complete file. Within this file, every individual sheet represents a separate tab.

The efficient management of spreadsheet tabs is a fundamental aspect of utilizing Google Sheets professionally. In this section, I will demonstrate the process of inserting new tabs, removing tabs, changing tab names, and arranging tabs in Google Sheets. While adding and deleting tabs are routine tasks, the significance of renaming and organizing tabs is often overlooked.

4.4.1 Adding a New Tab to Your Spreadsheet

To create an additional tab in Google Sheets, you can easily take the following actions:

- Located on the bottom-left area of your spreadsheet, next to the existing tab names, there is a plus sign labeled "Add Sheet." Simply click on it.
- Alternatively, you can opt for another approach by clicking on "Insert" in the toolbar menu at the top and then selecting "New Sheet."

4.4.2 Renaming a Tab in a Spreadsheet

If you're looking to change the name of a tab in Google Sheets, here's what you need to do:

- Give the tab a double-click or right-click on the tab name. Alternatively, you can click on the little

triangle located to the right of the tab name and select "Rename."
- Input the new name you want for the tab.
- Hit the "Enter" key on your keyboard to confirm the name change.

4.4.3 Remove a Tab from Your Spreadsheet

To remove a tab from Google Sheets, you can easily do so by following these simple steps:

- Simply right-click on the tab you would like to remove or click on the tiny triangle located to the left of the tab's name.
- A menu will appear, where you can select the option "Delete."

4.4.4 How to Reorder Your Tabs

If you want to rearrange the tabs in your spreadsheet, here's how you can do it:

- Select the tab you want to move by clicking on it near the tab name.
- Hold the click and drag your cursor either to the left or right, depending on where you want to place the tab.
- Once you've reached the desired location, let go of the click, and the tab will be moved to its new location.

Chapter 5: Data Sharing and Collaboration

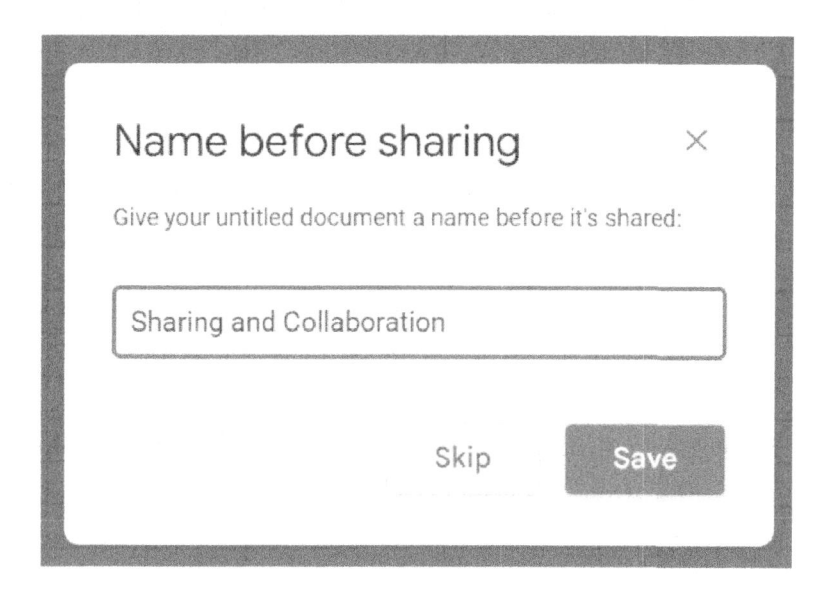

> **Name before sharing** ×
>
> Give your untitled document a name before it's shared:
>
> Sharing and Collaboration
>
> Skip   **Save**

5.1 Sharing with Specific Persons

Different sharing options are available, and these depend on the size of your group. For groups of up to 100 people, you have the flexibility to give view, edit, or comment permissions to multiple individuals concurrently when working on a Google Sheets file. However, when the group size exceeds 100 people, only the owner and select users with editing permissions can make changes to the file. To allow more than 100 people to access your file simultaneously, consider publishing it as a web page instead.

- Pick the spreadsheet file you would like to share.
- Hit the share option.
- Enter the Google group or email address you intend to grant access to.

- Choose the role of each person—viewer, commenter, or editor—for the spreadsheet file.
- If your account qualifies, you can control their access by adding an expiration date.
- Decide whether or not to notify the recipients.

a) To inform them about the shared item, mark the Notify People box. Each email address you enter will receive a notification.

b) If you prefer not to notify them, simply untick the box.

- Hit the Send or Share button.
- Select Share to bring up the window for adding people, then hit Send.

5.2 Restricting Access to Your Spreadsheet

If you're looking to control who can access your Google Sheets spreadsheet, here's a simple guide:

- Locate the desired folder or file within Google Sheets.
- Open or choose the specific folder or file you would like to restrict access to.
- Select the Share option and then click on the Copy link.
- Within the "General Access" section, click on the downward arrow.
- Choose the option labeled Restricted.
- Finally, click on the Done button to complete the process.

5.3 Unsharing a Spreadsheet File

- Locate the desired folder or file within Google Sheets.
- Access the folder or file by opening or selecting it.
- Navigate to the Share option and click on it.
- Identify the individual with whom you intend to discontinue sharing.
- Just beside their name, click on the downward arrow on the right and click on Remove access.
- Save your changes to complete the process.

5.4 Sharing a Link to Your Spreadsheet

In deciding who can access your file, you have the option to make it available to everyone or limit it to specific individuals. If you opt for unrestricted access via a shared link, there won't be any limitations on who can view the contents of your file.

- Choose the file you would like to share.
- Click on the Share option.
- Look for the "General Access" section and tap the dropdown arrow.
- Decide who gets to access the file.
- Determine the level of control individuals will have over your file by selecting Viewer, Commenter, or Editor.
- Finally, click Done to complete the process.

5.5 Chatting with Collaborators in Google Sheets

In order to engage in real-time conversations with your fellow collaborators within a Google Sheet, follow these simple steps:

- Begin by opening the desired spreadsheet on your computer.
- Look towards the upper right area of the screen and locate the "Show chat" option. Please note that this option will only appear if you are not the sole user of the file.
- Quick tip: If there are multiple collaborators, you will see a blue circle beside their avatars, indicating the number of extra participants. By clicking on this circle, you can access the chat by selecting "Join chat."
- Input your message into the chat box.
- Once you have completed the conversation, click on the "Close" button situated at the upper right area of the chat window.

Remember, it's important to keep in mind that all chats within Google Sheets are visible to anyone who has access to the file. Additionally, it's worth noting that these chats are not saved for future reference.

5.6 Different Methods for Tracking Changes in Google Sheets

When it comes to collaborating in Google Sheets, there are various methods available to keep track of changes. Let's explore a few of these options:

5.6.1 Using Version History to Track Google Sheet Changes

If you're looking to keep track of possible changes made to your Google Sheets using the version history, here's a simple guide to help you do just that:

- Start by accessing the "File" tab in your Google Sheets.
- From there, proceed to the "Version History" drop-down menu and click on "See version history."
- This will bring up a window where you can view all the previous versions of your spreadsheet.
- To track changes, simply click on any previous version listed in the version history.

5.6.1.1 Restoring from a Previous Version

- If you decide that you want to revert to a previous version, click on "Restore this version."
- Finally, click on "Restore" to confirm and revert your current version back to the earlier one.

5.6.2 Enabling Notification Rules to Track Google Sheet Changes

To keep track of changes in your Google Sheets, follow these steps:

- Open your Google Sheets and go to the "Tools" tab.
- From there, click on "Notification Settings" and select "Edit Notifications."
- In the "Set Notification Rules" box, you'll find different options for notification rules. Choose the one that best suits your requirements and click "Save."
- Once you've set a notification rule, simply hit the "Done" option.

Now, suppose someone makes changes to your Google Sheets. Gmail will automatically notify you about these changes.

5.6.3 Using Cell Edit History to Track Changes

In Google Sheets, keeping tabs on cell edits is a simple task.

- To begin, simply right-click on the desired cell.
- From the context menu that is displayed, choose the option that reads "Show edit history."
- A new window, labeled "Edit History," will be shown. Within this window, you'll find the ability to navigate between previous versions of the cell by clicking on the arrow-back or the previous edit option.

5.7 Using Comments While Collaborating in Google Sheets

When working online with programs like Google Sheets, you have access to comments, which is a very helpful feature. These writings provide a helpful way to address issues, clarify details, and foster collaboration within the boundaries of the spreadsheet.

With its flexible comment option, Google Sheets gives users the necessary resources to promote efficient teamwork on their next spreadsheet.

5.7.1 Adding a Comment to Your Sheet

Adding a comment to a spreadsheet is a simple process. Here's how you can do it:

- Begin by choosing the cell you would like to comment on. If you select multiple cells, a row, or a column, the comment will be linked to the first cell in the selection. To proceed, right-click on the cell or go to the menu bar and select "Insert," followed by "Comment."
- Once the comment box pops up, simply enter your note. If necessary, you can use the @ symbol to mention a particular user.
- Finally, click on "Comment" to save your comment.

5.7.2 How to View a Comment

Once you've successfully added a comment in Google Sheets, you'll notice a tiny triangular indicator in the upper-right area of the cell it's attached to.

- To view the comment, simply position your cursor over the cell. This handy feature will give you access to the comments associated with specific cells in your spreadsheet.

5.7.3 Taking Action on a Comment

When you add a comment to a cell in Google Sheets, it opens up a world of possibilities. Just like in Google Docs, comments in Google Sheets come with a range of actions that you can take. So if you're already familiar with comments in Google Docs, you'll feel right at home using them in Google Sheets.

5.7.4 Linking, Deleting, and Editing a Comment

If you are the author of a comment, you have the ability to include a link, erase the comment, or modify it by selecting the three dots located in the upper right corner. However, if you're reviewing a comment made by a collaborator who has access to the same document, you'll only have the option to create a link to the comment within this section.

5.7.5 Replying to a Comment

Interacting with comments is an essential part of the collaborative experience while using Google Sheets. Whether you're responding to your own comment or engaging with someone else's, the process is quite easy.

- To get started, just click on any text in the comment box. As you click, the reply area will smoothly expand in front of you.

- Once you've finished writing your response, all it takes is one click on "Reply" to send it.
- From that point on, whenever you place your cursor over the comment cell, you'll be met with the original comment and any replies that have been added below it.

5.7.6 How to Resolve Your Comment

Some comments serve as brief reminders or temporary annotations. They may be a prompt for a swift adjustment you would like to make. Once you have addressed a comment, simply tap the green checkmark. This action not only marks the comment as resolved but also conceals it along with its associated replies. Moreover, it eliminates the indicator located in the corner of the cell.

This feature grants you the ability to neatly store away resolved comments. However, there is no cause for concern. You can easily revisit and even reopen these comments by accessing the comments sidebar.

5.7.7 How to Use the Comments Sidebar

In addition to the convenient feature of being able to add, view, and respond to comments directly within a cell, there is another useful tool at your disposal: The Comments sidebar.

Accessing the sidebar is easy, as there are two simple methods to choose from:

- Firstly, you can open the sidebar by selecting a comment within the sheet, clicking on the comment

text, and then selecting "Open All Comments" at the bottom of the screen.
- Otherwise, you can click on the Open Comment History symbol located in the upper right corner of the workbook.

5.8 Sharing Your Sheets with Non-Gmail Users

Google provides a helpful feature called "visitor sharing" that allows organizations to enable document collaboration. With this option, visitors can access, comment on, or edit your document for a period of 7 days after verifying their email. To activate this sharing option, it is recommended that you reach out to your Google account administrator.

If you're looking to keep your documents private from visitors, here's a helpful guide on sharing files with users who don't have a Google account:

- To begin, locate the "Share" button positioned at the upper-right corner of the spreadsheet.
- Proceed to access the "Get link" section and choose the option that allows access to "Anyone with the link".
- Now, it's time to determine the sharing permissions for your Google Sheets. You have the choice between three levels: viewer, commenter, or editor.
- Once you have made your selection, simply copy the link and share it with the intended recipient, who does not have a Google account.

Chapter 6: Modern Data Analysis Methods

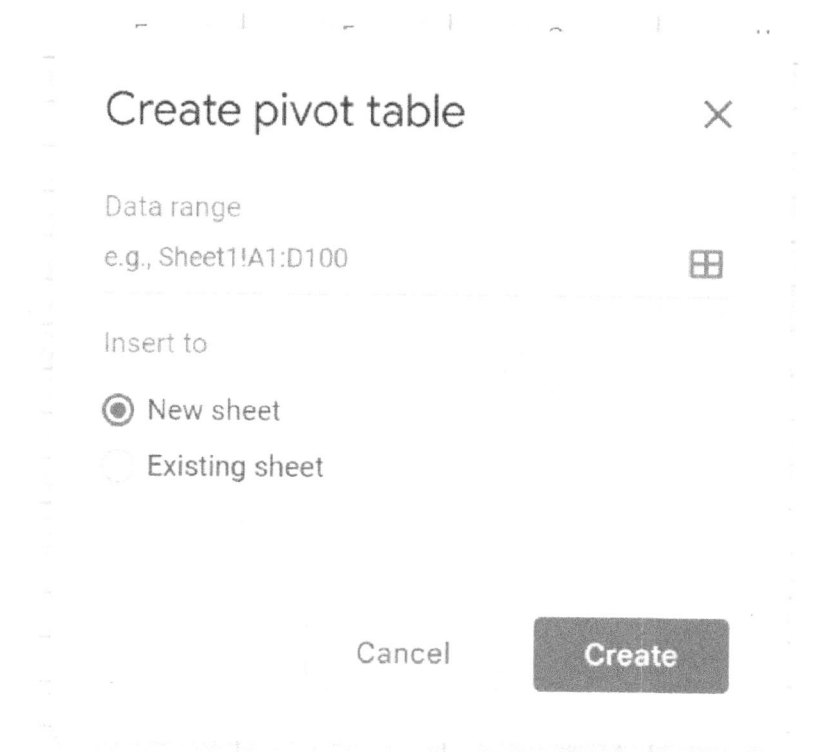

Create pivot table

Data range
e.g., Sheet1!A1:D100

Insert to

◉ New sheet

○ Existing sheet

Cancel   **Create**

6.1 Data Analysis from a Various Approach Using Pivot Tables

Spreadsheet programs are undoubtedly useful for analyzing data, but at times, they can leave us yearning for a deeper understanding. When faced with a vast amount of information, it becomes challenging to condense and derive meaningful insights from a simple spreadsheet layout.

Enter pivot tables, the secret weapon of Excel fans. But if you are a Google Sheets user, don't lose hope. You can also have an ally in pivot tables.

I'll walk you through the process of making pivot tables in Google Sheets step by step in this section.

6.2 What are Pivot Tables?

A pivot table is a powerful tool for summarizing large sets of data, typically found in spreadsheets. While small data sets can be easily comprehended by scanning through them, larger spreadsheets require a more efficient approach to drawing meaningful conclusions. This is where pivot tables prove their worth.

To understand their functionality, envision traditional spreadsheets as having "flat data," organized along two axes: rows (vertical) and columns (horizontal).

Imagine a table where every sale is neatly displayed in its own row, with various columns offering specific details about that particular sale. However, if you wish to delve deeper and uncover more meaningful insights, you need to introduce another layer of data. This can be achieved by shifting or pivoting the axes of the table. Instead of focusing on individual sales, you can now examine aggregated data, such as the number of units sold by each sales representative for each product. Essentially, this involves transforming a two-dimensional table into a three-dimensional one, thereby expanding the possibilities of analysis.

Despite the fact that you could derive a lot of these insights using formulas, the pivot table allows you to summarize them in a much shorter amount of time—and with a smaller likelihood of human error. By doing this, rather than having to start from scratch each time a client or your company requests a fresh report based on the exact same data set, you can put it together with just a couple of clicks.

6.2.1 Creating Your First Pivot Table

Here's a brief guide on utilizing a Google Sheets pivot table.

- Launch a spreadsheet in Google Sheets.
- Highlight every cell containing the data source you would like to utilize; these should include the column headers.
- Access the "Insert" option, click on it, and then choose "Pivot table".
- A panel called "Create pivot table" will be displayed. Decide whether you want to insert the pivot table into a brand new sheet or an existing one. Next, hit "Create".
- In the "Pivot Table Editor" panel, you'll find the options for rows and columns. Click "Add" beside each one to select the data you want to analyze.
- Within the same panel, locate "Values" and select "Add" to choose the values you wish to show within the columns and rows.
- To show only specific criteria-based values, you can apply filters.

Your pivot table's data will automatically update whenever the source data undergoes changes. In case you don't immediately observe these adjustments in your pivot table, simply refresh the page. The update process might require a few moments, depending on the extent of the data alterations.

6.2.2 Editing a Pivot Table

A pivot table editor panel will show up right away when Google Sheets first fills your pivot table. To create different kinds of reports, you need to customize your pivot table.

6.2.2.1 Relaunching the Pivot Table Editor Panel

Hover over the pivot table and select Edit to reopen the editor after it has been closed.

Quick Tip: The editor provides two options for data analysis: manually selecting your table dimensions or using Google Sheets' suggestions.

6.3 Customizing Your Pivot Table

Google Sheets gives you the option to change the summary, sorting, listing, or filtering of the data in your pivot table.

6.3.1 Changing the Header Name of Your Pivot Table

To modify a column header, follow these steps:

- Access Google Sheets on your computer and open the desired spreadsheet.
- Locate the pivot table and click on the "Edit" button that appears as a pop-up below it.
- Identify the specific column or row whose header you would like to change, and simply click on its name.
- Then, enter a new name of your choice.

When working with Google Sheets, it's important to be aware of how field renaming affects pivot tables. If you decide to rename a field in Sheets after creating a pivot table, you'll notice that the field is automatically renamed in the pivot table editor as well. The new name is a combination of the previous field name and the new name enclosed in parentheses. For instance, if you rename "price per unit" to "average price" in the pivot table editor, the field will be displayed as "price per unit (average price)" in the pivot table editor. However, it's worth noting that you cannot rename the "Grand Total" field.

6.3.2 Sorting and Ordering Rows or Columns

In Google Sheets, you have the ability to organize and arrange your data using pivot tables. Take the following steps to do just that:

- Start by opening the desired spreadsheet on your computer using Google Sheets.
- Locate the pivot table and click on the Edit button that appears as a pop-up.
- Within the "Rows" or "Columns" section, find the "Sort by" or "Order" option and click on the arrow beside it.

Note: If you would like to display the totals for a particular column or row, simply tick the box labeled "Show totals."

6.4 Grouping Pivot Table Data Together

A pivot table's values can be selected and manually or automatically grouped together using a rule.

6.4.1 Grouping Rows Together by a Rule

- Start by opening the desired spreadsheet on your computer using Google Sheets.
- Locate the pivot table and click on the Edit button that appears as a pop-up.
- Continue by performing a right-click on a cell, followed by selecting the option to create a pivot group rule.
- If you are dealing with numerical data, you have the flexibility to choose an interval size. Additionally, there is an optional feature that allows you to specify the starting and ending points for your groups.
- Once you have made the necessary adjustments, simply click the OK button to finalize the process.

6.4.2 Manual Grouping

- Start by opening the desired spreadsheet on your computer using Google Sheets.
- Locate the pivot table and click on the Edit button that appears as a pop-up.
- Continue by right-clicking on the cells, then choose the option to create a pivot group.
- Next, carefully select the cells that you wish to group together.

6.4.3 Grouping Rows Together by Date or Time

- Start by opening the desired spreadsheet on your computer using Google Sheets.
- Locate the pivot table and click on the Edit button that appears as a pop-up.
- Select Create pivot date group from the context menu after right-clicking a cell that has date-formatted content.
- Select a date or period of time to group by.

6.4.4 Ungrouping Items in a Pivot Table

- Right-click any grouped item.
- Next, select Ungroup pivot items to ungroup them.

6.5 Filtering Pivot Table Data

Data that you do not want displayed in your table can be hidden.

- Open the spreadsheet containing your pivot table on your computer.
- Locate the Edit button beneath the pivot table and click on it.
- On the right-hand side, find the "Filters" section and click on "Add."
- Then, click on the downward-facing arrow beside the "Showing all items" option.
- You have two options for filtering:
a) Filter by condition: You can either create your own condition or choose from a list of predefined conditions. For example, you can filter based on

whether a cell is empty, if the data is below a certain value, or if a specific letter or phrase is present in the text.
b) Filter by values: If you want to hide specific items, simply uncheck them and click "OK."

When it comes to working with pivot tables, it's important to keep a few things in mind. Firstly, if you choose to filter your data by value and then make changes to the source data, you will have to update the filter in your pivot table in order to reflect those changes. Secondly, if you decide to filter by condition, you have the flexibility to enter a cell reference, a specific value, or even a field from your data. For instance, if you opt for the "greater than" condition, you can input a value such as 25, a cell reference like =Sheet1!B1, or a field name like =Sales (assuming your data includes a field named Sales).

6.6 How to Use Advanced Functions for Data Analysis

Data analytics is a vast and complex field of study. Experts attempt to extract useful insights and identify patterns inside large datasets using complex computing methods and detailed statistical models.

Data analytics is really about getting meaning out of data. Spreadsheets are capable of organizing financial data and computing costs, but they cannot fully explain all of their implications on their own.

One can find interesting spots in the data and make inferences by using a variety of functions to compare and filter it. For instance, a quick glance may disclose the best-performing goods in a company's portfolio, but data analysis is required to identify the products that are expanding and making significant profits.

In the end, data analysts work to comprehend the underlying factors that contribute to the data and to put together a comprehensive grasp of the wider picture.

6.6.1 Advanced Functions in Google Sheets

In spreadsheets, there are a few functions that have become household names, such as SUM, COUNT, and AVERAGE. These trusty tools serve us well in a variety of situations. But when it comes to diving deep into data analysis, a little extra firepower is needed. Thankfully, spreadsheet applications like Google Sheets are equipped with a range of functions tailored specifically for analytics. Let's dive in.

6.6.2 ABS

The ABS function, often overlooked in spreadsheet operations, serves as a valuable tool for those familiar with mathematical concepts. Functionally resembling the modulo function, it offers a way to obtain the absolute value of a number, disregarding any distinction between positive and negative values.

In essence, applying the ABS function to a group of cells comprising various numbers generates a consistently positive range. This uniformity only varies in terms of magnitude rather than polarity. Although seemingly insignificant, this feature holds significant importance when incorporating data from multiple columns into intricate calculations, as sporadic negative values can disrupt the accuracy of the results.

6.6.3 SUMIF

SUMIF adds up values within a range that satisfy a certain requirement. The syntax for SUMIF is =SUMIF(range, criterion, [sum_range])

6.6.4 VLOOKUP

Finding the right information is a crucial aspect of analytics. While it may not be challenging when dealing with a single sheet containing only a few entries, things get complicated when you have extensive projects spread across multiple spreadsheets with numerous lines of data. In such cases, a more efficient method of searching becomes necessary.

This is where the VLOOKUP formula comes into play. VLOOKUP, short for 'vertical lookup,' allows you to search for a specific value in vertical columns. To streamline VLOOKUP operations, it is recommended to use columns as fields.

However, there is a limitation to VLOOKUP. It requires an exact match, so if you're looking for an approximate match, this function won't be suitable.

6.6.5 COUNTIF

With the COUNTIF function, you can figure out how many cells in the selected range satisfy a defined

requirement. The syntax for COUNTIF is
=COUNTIF(range, criterion).

6.6.6 HLOOKUP

This function looks up a value in the first row of a range and returns the value from the selected row. The syntax for HLOOKUP is
=HLOOKUP(search_key, range, row_index, [is_sorted])

6.6.7 MATCH and INDEX

The MATCH function is a valuable tool when it comes to locating cells that contain an approximate or specific value within a spreadsheet. Its primary function is to determine the relative position of the target cell within a given range, making it particularly useful for sorting through data sets.

However, when combined with the INDEX function, MATCH truly shines as a more dynamic alternative to the VLOOKUP formula. Unlike VLOOKUP, INDEX not only provides the value of a specified cell index but also allows you to determine the index of the desired value itself. By leveraging both functions, users can effortlessly search for values within a range throughout the entire spreadsheet, expanding the possibilities of data analysis and retrieval.

6.6.8 AVERAGEIF

AVERAGEIF: This function determines the mean of values falling within a range and satisfying a particular requirement. The syntax for AVERAGEIF is
=AVERAGEIF(range, criterion, [average_range]).

Chapter 7: Harnessing the Power of Macros and Scripts

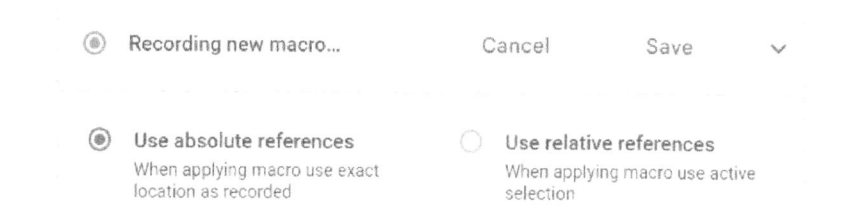

- ● Recording new macro...   Cancel   Save   ˅

- ● **Use absolute references**
  When applying macro use exact location as recorded
- ○ **Use relative references**
  When applying macro use active selection

7.1 Automating Tasks with Macros

A macro presents a simple solution for automating repetitive tasks within Google Sheets. By recording a sequence of actions, you can conveniently reuse them in the future with a single click. The beauty of macros lies in their ability to leverage the power of Google Apps Script, even without any coding knowledge.

To illustrate, imagine you're constructing a basic compound interest calculator in Google Sheets. This calculator requires three input parameters, such as the interest rate, time period, and principal amount. The desired output will be the resulting amount at maturity.

Before sharing this spreadsheet with your family and friends, you'd like to ensure that the input and output cells are clearly formatted. This way, they'll easily identify which cells they can modify according to their own requirements.

To achieve this, you devise a formatting method:
- Input cells will feature a light yellow background with dark gray text that appears bold.
- The output cell will have a light green background, accompanied by dark green text that is also bold.

Given that there are three input cells, applying the same formatting rules repeatedly would become tedious. Instead, by recording these formatting steps as a macro initially, you can effortlessly apply them in the future with just a single click.

7.2 Recording a Macro in a Google Sheet

To set up a macro in Google Sheets, follow these steps:

- Begin by opening a spreadsheet on your computer at sheets.google.com.
- Find the Extensions option at the top of the page and click on it. From there, select Macros and then choose the Record macro option.
- When you get to the bottom of the page, you'll be prompted to decide on the type of cell reference you prefer for your macro:
a) You can opt for absolute references, which means the recorded macro will perform tasks exclusively on the specific cell you initially selected. For example, if you bold cell C3, the macro will always apply the formatting to that exact cell, regardless of any subsequent cell selections.
b) Alternatively, you can choose relative references. In this case, the macro will execute tasks on the initially selected cell and its neighboring cells. For instance, if

you record the process of bolding cells E1 and F1, the macro can be later used to bold cells G1 and H1.
- Carry out the task that you intend to record using the macro. Once you're finished, click on the Save button.
- Provide a name for the macro, create a custom shortcut if desired, and then save the changes.

Note: Keep in mind that creating a macro in Google Sheets generates an Apps Script. To edit this script, click on the Tools option at the top of the page and then select Script Editor.

7.2.1 Executing a Macro

- To execute a macro, go to the Extensions option,
- Choose Macros, and select the specific macro you want to run.

7.2.2 Using an Earlier Recorded Macro

If you're looking to apply a macro that you've previously recorded to a specific range or cell, the process is quite simple.

- Begin by selecting the desired range or cell where you want the macro to take effect.
- Next, navigate to the Tools menu and choose Macros.
- From the list of available macros, select the one you want to apply.

It's worth noting that when you run a macro for the first time, Google Sheets will prompt you to grant access to your spreadsheet as a security measure. Once you've done that, a single click is all it takes to format the selected cell or range according to the macro.

7.2.3 Viewing Auto-Generated Code for Your Macros

Macros serve as automated Google scripts that are conveniently generated on your behalf. In other words, when you record a macro, Google Sheets takes the liberty of creating a Google Apps script tailored to your actions.

- To access the auto-generated code, navigate to Tools.
- Select Macros, and then choose Manage macros.
- From there, opt to edit the script via the three-dot menu.

If you're looking to learn about Apps Script functionality, a handy trick is to record a macro while manually making changes and study the automatically generated Apps Script code.

7.3 Editing a Macro

You have the power to customize your experience by modifying the name, assigning a shortcut, adjusting the script, or deleting a macro.

- Access sheets.google.com on your computer.
- Proceed to the top and select Extensions, followed by Macros, and then click on Manage macros.

- Implement your desired modifications. To eliminate a macro or modify the script, locate the targeted macro and click on the "More" option.
- Finalize your changes by clicking on the Update button.

7.4 How to Schedule a Macro

In order to automate tasks in Google Sheets, you have the flexibility to customize your macros based on various triggers. These triggers can be set to activate the macro according to specific actions, a designated date or time, time intervals, or updates in your calendar. To get started, follow these steps:

- Access sheets.google.com on your computer and open the desired spreadsheet.
- Navigate to the "Tools" menu and select "Script editor."
- In the script editor window, click on "Edit" and then choose "Current project's triggers."
- At the lower right corner, you'll find an option to "Add trigger." Click on it and configure your desired trigger settings.
- Once you've customized the trigger, don't forget to click "Save" to apply the changes.

7.5 Importing Custom Google App Script Functions

You have the option to incorporate personalized functions created with the Google Apps script into your projects.

- Access sheets.google.com on your computer and open a spreadsheet.
- Click on Extensions at the top, followed by Macros, and then click on Import macro.
- Select the desired function you would like to import and click on Add function next to it.

Chapter 8: Tricks and Strategies for Efficiency

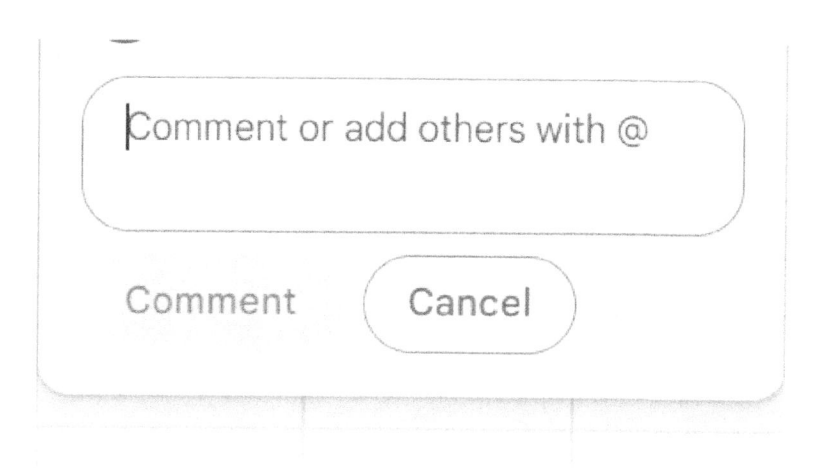

8.1 Keyboard Shortcuts for Google Sheets

You can harness the power of keyboard shortcuts in Google Sheets to seamlessly navigate, format, and utilize formulas. It's worth noting that certain shortcuts may not be applicable to all languages or keyboard layouts.

To access a comprehensive list of keyboard shortcuts in Google Sheets, simply press Ctrl + / on Chrome OS and Windows, or ⌘ + / on Mac. For those looking for the tool finder (formerly known as menu search), you can find it by pressing Alt + / on Chrome OS and Windows, or Option + / on Mac.

8.1.1 Common Google Sheet Actions

Selecting All

for PC: Ctrl+a or Ctrl+Shift+Space

for Mac: ⌘+a or ⌘+Shift+Space
for Chrome OS: Ctrl+a

Selecting Row
for PC: Shift+Space
for Mac: Shift+Space
for Chrome OS: Shift+Space

Selecting Column
for PC: Ctrl+Space
for Mac: Ctrl+Space
for Chrome OS: Ctrl+Space

Find
for PC: Ctrl+f

for Mac: ⌘+f
for Chrome OS: Ctrl+f

Finding and Replacing Items
for PC: Ctrl+h

for Mac: ⌘+Shift+h
for Chrome OS: Ctrl+h

Undo
for PC: Ctrl+z

for Mac: ⌘+z
for Chrome OS: Ctrl+z

Redo
for PC: Ctrl+y, Ctrl+Shift+z, or F4.

for Mac: ⌘+y, or ⌘+Shift+z, or Fn+F4
for Chrome OS: Ctrl+y or Ctrl+Shift+z

Fill Down
for PC: Ctrl+d
for Mac: ⌘+d
for Chrome OS: Ctrl+d

Fill Range
for PC: Ctrl+Enter
for Mac: ⌘+Enter
for Chrome OS: Ctrl+Enter

Fill Right
for PC: Ctrl+r
for Mac: ⌘+r
for Chrome OS: Ctrl+r

Open
for PC: Ctrl+o
for Mac: ⌘+o
for Chrome OS: Ctrl+o

Saving a Sheet
for PC: Ctrl+s
for Mac: ⌘+s
for Chrome OS: Ctrl+s

Copying an Item
for PC: Ctrl+c

for Mac: ⌘+c
for Chrome OS: Ctrl+c

Pasting an Item
for PC: Ctrl+v

for Mac: ⌘+v
for Chrome OS: Ctrl+v

Paste Values Only
for PC: Ctrl+Shift+v

for Mac: ⌘+Shift+v
for Chrome OS: Ctrl+Shift+v

Cutting an Item
for PC: Ctrl+x

for Mac: ⌘+x
for Chrome OS: Ctrl+x

Printing a Sheet
for PC: Ctrl+p

for Mac: ⌘+p
for Chrome OS: Ctrl+p

Showing Common Keyboard Shortcuts
for PC: Ctrl+/

for Mac: ⌘+/
for Chrome OS: Ctrl+/

Compacting Controls
for PC: Ctrl+Shift+f

for Mac: Ctrl+Shift+f
for Chrome OS: Ctrl+Shift+f

Inserting a New Sheet
for PC: Shift+F11
for Mac: Shift+Fn+F11

Selecting Input Tools
for PC: Ctrl+Alt+Shift+k

for Mac: ⌘+Option+Shift+k
for Chrome OS: Ctrl+Alt+Shift+k

Input Tools On/Off (available in spreadsheets in non-Latin languages)
for PC: Ctrl+Shift+k

for Mac: ⌘+Shift+k
for Chrome OS: Ctrl+Shift+k

Searching the Menus
for PC: Alt+/
for Mac: Option+/
for Chrome OS: Alt+/

8.1.2 Shortcuts for Formatting Cells

Bold
for PC: Ctrl+b

for Mac: ⌘+b
for Chrome OS: Ctrl+b

Italic

for PC: Ctrl+i

for Mac: ⌘+i

for Chrome OS: Ctrl+i

Underline
for PC: Ctrl+u

for Mac: ⌘+u

for Chrome OS: Ctrl+u

Strikethrough
for PC: Alt+Shift+5
for Mac: Option+Shift+5
for Chrome OS: Alt+Shift+5

Left Align
for PC: Ctrl+Shift+l

for Mac: ⌘+Shift+l
for Chrome OS: Ctrl+Shift+l

Center Align
for PC: Ctrl+Shift+e

for Mac: ⌘+Shift+e
for Chrome OS: Ctrl+Shift+e

Right Align
for PC: Ctrl+Shift+r

for Mac: ⌘+Shift+r
for Chrome OS: Ctrl+Shift+r

Applying the Right Border

for PC: Alt+Shift+2
for Mac: Option+Shift+2
for Chrome OS: Alt+Shift+2

Applying the Top Border
for PC: Alt+Shift+1
for Mac: Option+Shift+1
for Chrome OS: Alt+Shift+1

Applying the Left Border
for PC: Alt+Shift+4
for Mac: Option+Shift+4
for Chrome OS: Alt+Shift+4

Applying the Bottom Border
for PC: Alt+Shift+3
for Mac: Option+Shift+3
for Chrome OS: Alt+Shift+3

Applying the Outer Border
for PC: Alt+Shift+7 or Ctrl+Shift+7

for Mac: Option+Shift+7 or ⌘+Shift+7
for Chrome OS: Alt+Shift+7 or Ctrl+Shift+7

Removing Borders
for PC: Alt+Shift+6
for Mac: Option+Shift+6
for Chrome OS: Alt+Shift+6

Inserting Time
for PC: Ctrl+Shift+;

for Mac: ⌘+Shift+;
for Chrome OS: Ctrl+Shift+;

Inserting Link
for PC: Ctrl+k

for Mac: ⌘+k
for Chrome OS: Ctrl+k

Insert Date and Time
for PC: Ctrl+Alt+Shift+;

for Mac: ⌘+Option+Shift+;
for Chrome OS: Ctrl+Alt+Shift+;

Inserting Date
for PC: Ctrl+;

for Mac: ⌘+;
for Chrome OS: Ctrl+;

Format as Decimal
for PC: Ctrl+Shift+1
for Mac: Ctrl+Shift+1
for Chrome OS: Ctrl+Shift+1

Format as Date
for PC: Ctrl+Shift+3
for Mac: Ctrl+Shift+3
for Chrome OS: Ctrl+Shift+3

Format as Time
for PC: Ctrl+Shift+2
for Mac: Ctrl+Shift+2
for Chrome OS: Ctrl+Shift+2

Format as a Percentage
for PC: Ctrl+Shift+5
for Mac: Ctrl+Shift+5
for Chrome OS: Ctrl+Shift+5

Format as Currency
for PC: Ctrl+Shift+4
for Mac: Ctrl+Shift+4
for Chrome OS: Ctrl+Shift+4

Format as an Exponent
for PC: Ctrl+Shift+6
for Mac: Ctrl+Shift+6
for Chrome OS: Ctrl+Shift+6

Clear Formatting
for PC: Ctrl+\

for Mac: ⌘+\

for Chrome OS: Ctrl+\

8.1.3 Navigating a Spreadsheet

Moving to the Beginning of the Sheet
for PC: Ctrl+Home

for Mac: ⌘+Fn+Left Arrow

for Chrome OS: Ctrl+Search+Left Arrow

Moving to the Start of the Row
for PC: Home
for Mac: Fn+Left Arrow
for Chrome OS: Search+Left Arrow

Moving to the End of the Sheet
for PC: Ctrl+End
for Mac: ⌘+Fn+Right Arrow
for Chrome OS: Ctrl+Search+Right Arrow

Moving to the End of the Row
for PC: End
for Mac: Fn+Right Arrow
for Chrome OS: Search+Right Arrow

Scrolling to an Active Cell
for PC: Ctrl+Backspace
for Mac: ⌘+Backspace
for Chrome OS: Ctrl+Backspace

Moving to the Previous Sheet
for PC: Alt+Up Arrow
for Mac: Option+Up Arrow
for Chrome OS: Ctrl+Shift+Search+Up Arrow

Moving to the Next Sheet
for PC: Alt+Down Arrow
for Mac: Option+Down Arrow
for Chrome OS: Ctrl+Shift+Search+Down Arrow

Displaying a List of Sheets
for PC: Alt+Shift+k
for Mac: Option+Shift+k
for Chrome OS: Alt+Shift+k

Opening Explore
for PC: Alt+Shift+x
for Mac: Option+Shift+x

for Chrome OS: Alt+Shift+x

Opening a Hyperlink
for PC: Alt+Enter
for Mac: Option+Enter
for Chrome OS: Alt+Enter

Proceeding to the Side Panel
for PC: Ctrl+Alt+. or Ctrl+Alt+,

for Mac: ⌘+Option+. ⌘+Option+,
for Chrome OS: Alt+Shift+. or Alt+Shift+,

Moving to Quicksum (when a range of cells is selected)
for PC: Alt+Shift+q
for Mac: Option+Shift+q
for Chrome OS: Alt+Shift+q

Moving Focus Out of the Spreadsheet
for PC: Ctrl+Alt+Shift+m

for Mac: Ctrl+⌘+Shift+m
for Chrome OS: Ctrl+Alt+Shift+m

Moving Focus to Popup (for images, bookmarks, and links)
for PC: Ctrl+Alt+e,p
for Mac: Ctrl++e,p
for Chrome OS: Ctrl+Alt+e,p

Opening Revision History
for PC: Ctrl+Alt+Shift+h

for Mac: ⌘+Option+Shift+h
for Chrome OS: Ctrl+Alt+Shift+h

Opening the Dropdown Menu on a Filtered Cell
for PC: Ctrl+Alt+r

for Mac: Ctrl+⌘+r
for Chrome OS: Ctrl+Alt+r

Opening Chat Inside a Spreadsheet
for PC: Shift+Esc
for Mac: Shift+Esc
for Chrome OS: Shift+Esc

Closing Drawing Editor
for PC: Shift+Esc

for Mac: ⌘+Esc or Shift+Esc
for Chrome OS: Ctrl+Esc or Shift+Esc

Moving to the Top Left of the Sheet
for Chrome OS: Ctrl+Search+Left Arrow

Moving to the Bottom Right of the Sheet
for Chrome OS: Ctrl+Search+Right Arrow

Moving to the Last Cell in the Row that Contains Data
for Chrome OS: Ctrl+Right Arrow

Moving to the First Cell in the Row that Contains Data
for Chrome OS: Ctrl+Left Arrow

8.1.4 Editing Comments and Notes

Inserting or Editing a Comment
for PC: Ctrl+Alt+m

for Mac: ⌘+Option+m
for Chrome OS: Ctrl+Alt+m

Inserting or Editing a Note
for PC: Shift+F2
for Mac: Shift+F2
for Chrome OS: Shift+Search+2

Entering a Current Comment
for PC: Ctrl+Alt+e,c

for Mac: Ctrl+⌘+e,c

for Chrome OS: Ctrl+Alt+e,c

Opening a Comment Discussion Thread
for PC: Ctrl+Alt+Shift+a

for Mac: ⌘+Option+Shift+a
for Chrome OS: Ctrl+Alt+Shift+a

Moving to the Previous Comment
for PC: Ctrl+Alt+p,c

for Mac: Ctrl+⌘+p,c
for Chrome OS: Ctrl+Alt+p,c

Moving to the Next Comment
for PC: Ctrl+Alt+n,c

for Mac: Ctrl+⌘+n,c
for Chrome OS: Ctrl+Alt+n,c

8.1.5 Opening a Menu

File Menu
for PC: Alt+f in Google Chrome or Alt+Shift+f in other browsers
for Mac: Ctrl+Option+f
for Chrome OS: Alt+f

View Menu
for PC: Alt+v in Google Chrome or Alt+Shift+v in other browsers
for Mac: Ctrl+Option+v
for Chrome OS: Alt+v

Edit Menu
for PC: Alt+e in Google Chrome or Alt+Shift+e in other browsers
for Mac: Ctrl+Option+e
for Chrome OS: Alt+e

Format Menu
for PC: Alt+o in Google Chrome or Alt+Shift+o in other browsers
for Mac: Ctrl+Option+o
for Chrome OS: Alt+o

Insert Menu
for PC: Alt+i in Google Chrome or Alt+Shift+i in other browsers
for Mac: Ctrl+Option+i
for Chrome OS: Alt+i

Tools Menu
for PC: Alt+t in Google Chrome or Alt+Shift+t in other browsers
for Mac: Ctrl+Option+t
for Chrome OS: Alt+t

Data Menu
for PC: Alt+d in Google Chrome or Alt+Shift+d in other browsers
for Mac: Ctrl+Option+d
for Chrome OS: Alt+d

Opening the Delete Menu
for PC: Select the desired cells and press Ctrl+Alt+-

for Mac: Select the desired cells and press ⌘+Option+-

for Chrome OS: Select the desired cells and press Ctrl+Alt+-

Opening the Insert Menu
for PC: Select the desired cells and press Ctrl+Alt+Shift+= or Ctrl+Alt+=

for Mac: Select the desired cells and press ⌘+Option+=

for Chrome OS: Select the desired cells and press Ctrl+Alt+=

Add-ons Menu
for PC: Alt+n in Google Chrome or Alt+Shift+n in other browsers
for Mac: Ctrl+Option+n
for Chrome OS: Alt+n

Form Menu (this appears whenever your spreadsheet is linked to a form)
for PC: Alt+m in Google Chrome or Alt+Shift+m in other browsers
for Mac: Ctrl+Option+m
for Chrome OS: Alt+m

Accessibility Menu (This appears whenever you enable screen reader support.)
for PC: Alt+a in Google Chrome or Alt+Shift+a in other browsers
for Mac: Ctrl+Option+a
for Chrome OS: Alt+a

Help Menu
for PC: Alt+h in Google Chrome or Alt+Shift+h in other browsers
for Mac: Ctrl+Option+h
for Chrome OS: Alt+h

Context Menu
for PC: Ctrl+Shift+\

for Mac: ⌘+Shift+\
for Chrome OS: Ctrl+Shift+\

Sheet Menu (delete, copy, and other sheet actions)
for PC: Alt+Shift+s
for Mac: Option+Shift+s
for Chrome OS: Ctrl+Shift+s

8.1.6 Adding or Changing Columns and Rows

Inserting Columns to the Left
for PC: Ctrl+Alt+Shift+= or Ctrl+Alt+= or Alt+i,r in Google Chrome, or Alt+Shift+i,c in other browsers (while selecting desired columns)

for Mac: ⌘+Option+= or Ctrl+Option+i,c while selecting your desired columns
for Chrome OS: Ctrl+Alt+= or Alt+i,c while selecting your desired columns

Inserting Columns to the Right
for PC: Alt+i,o in Google Chrome, or Alt+Shift+i,o in other browsers
for Mac: Ctrl+Option+i,o
for Chrome OS: Alt+i,o

Inserting Rows Above
for PC: Ctrl+Alt+Shift+= or Ctrl+Alt+= or Alt+i,r in Google Chrome, or Alt+Shift+i,r in other browsers (while selecting the desired rows)

for Mac: ⌘+Option+= or Ctrl+Option+i,r while selecting your desired rows
for Chrome OS: Ctrl+Alt+= or Alt+i,r while selecting your desired rows.

Inserting Rows Below
for PC: Alt+i,b in Google Chrome, or Alt+Shift+i,b in other browsers
for Mac: Ctrl+Option+i,b
for Chrome OS: Alt+i,b

Deleting Columns

for PC: Ctrl+Alt+- or Alt+e,e in Google Chrome, or Alt+Shift+e,e in other browsers (while selecting the columns)

for Mac: Select the desired columns and press

⌘+Option+- or Ctrl+Option+e

for Chrome OS: Select the desired columns and press Ctrl+Alt+- or Alt+e

Deleting Rows

for PC: Ctrl+Alt+- or Alt+e,d in Google Chrome, or Alt+Shift+e,d in other browsers (while selecting the rows)

for Mac: Select the desired rows and press ⌘+Option+- or Ctrl+Option+e,d
for Chrome OS: Select the desired rows and press Ctrl+Alt+- or Alt+e,d

Hiding Columns

for PC: Ctrl+Alt+0

for Mac: ⌘+Option+0
for Chrome OS: Ctrl+Alt+0

Unhiding Columns

for PC: Ctrl+Shift+0

for Mac: ⌘+Shift+0
for Chrome OS: Ctrl+Shift+0

Hiding Rows

for PC: Ctrl+Alt+9

for Mac: ⌘+Option+9

for Chrome OS: Ctrl+Alt+9

Unhiding Rows
for PC: Ctrl+Shift+9

for Mac: ⌘+Shift+9
for Chrome OS: Ctrl+Shift+9

Expanding Grouped Column or Rows
for PC: Alt+Shift+Down Arrow
for Mac: Option+Shift+Down Arrow
for Chrome OS: Alt+Shift+Down Arrow

Collapsing Grouped Columns or Rows
for PC: Alt+Shift+Up Arrow
for Mac: Option+Shift+Up Arrow
for Chrome OS: Alt+Shift+Up Arrow

Grouping Columns or Rows
for PC: Alt+Shift+Right Arrow
for Mac: Option+Shift+Right Arrow
for Chrome OS: Alt+Shift+Right Arrow

Ungrouping Columns or Rows
for PC: Alt+Shift+Left Arrow
for Mac: Option+Shift+Left Arrow
for Chrome OS: Alt+Shift+Left Arrow

8.1.7 Using Formulas

Inserting an Array Formula
for PC: Ctrl+Shift+Enter

for Mac: ⌘+Shift+Enter
for Chrome OS: Ctrl+Shift+Enter

Collapsing an Expanded Array Formula
for PC: Ctrl+e
for Mac: ⌘+e
for Chrome OS: Ctrl+e

Revealing or Concealing Formula Help (when you enter a formula)
for PC: Shift+F1
for Mac: Shift+Fn+F1
for Chrome OS: Shift+Search+1

Revealing all Formulas
for PC: Ctrl+~
for Mac: Ctrl+~
for Chrome OS: Ctrl+~

Relative or Absolute References (when you enter a formula)
for PC: F4
for Mac: Fn+F4
for Chrome OS: Search+4

Full or Compact Formula Help (when you enter a formula)
for PC: F1
for Mac: Fn+F1
for Chrome OS: Search+1

Resizing the Formula Bar (going up or down)

for PC: Ctrl+Up or Ctrl+Down
for Mac: Ctrl+Option+Up or Ctrl+Option+Down
for Chrome OS: Ctrl+Shift+Up Arrow or Ctrl+Shift+Down Arrow

Toggle Formula Result Previews (when you enter a formula)
for PC: F9
for Mac: Fn+F9
for Chrome OS: Search+9

Chapter 9: Troubleshooting Common Problems and Errors

When it comes to resolving issues, troubleshooting is often the key. However, some problems may necessitate a reevaluation of your approach. If you find yourself unsure of how to tackle a specific issue, I have compiled a list of the most frequently encountered problems in Google Sheets, along with their corresponding solutions.

9.1 Categories of Common Issues

Encountering problems with Google Sheets can be quite frustrating since it may not be easy to pinpoint the underlying problem. The issue could be due to a weak internet connection or cache buildup in your browser. To help you identify the problem, here are some common problems you may face while working with spreadsheets using Google Sheets:

9.1.1 Spreadsheet Crash

Spreadsheet files can sometimes be a major source of frustration if they shut down unexpectedly or fail to open, causing inconvenience. Attempting to access the file often leads to Sheets returning to the homepage. However, the issue can be resolved by creating a copy of the file or using a different account.

9.1.2 Something Went Wrong

If you encounter this error while using Sheets, a notification will pop up in the top-middle section of your screen. This message will give you the option to reload the page. Usually, this error is caused by a poor internet connection.

9.1.3 A Network Error Has Occurred

Encountering a network error can be a common occurrence, particularly when using mobile applications. You may come across a disheartening message that suggests switching to Google Chrome for a more seamless experience.

9.1.4 Spreadsheet Keeps Loading

When you find yourself confronted with unresponsive spreadsheets, frustration can quickly set in. It's not uncommon to see a persistent "Still loading" message occupying the top-right area of your screen, effectively rendering every tab and menu inaccessible. This dilemma leaves you stranded, unable to make any progress or modifications to your sheets.

9.1.5 Access Denied Message

In this type of issue, permission to access your spreadsheet is denied. Sheets alerts you to the unfortunate fact that you lack the necessary authorization to make changes to a spreadsheet that is rightfully yours. Moreover, any modifications you attempt to make will not be saved until you are once again granted access to the document.

9.2 Basic Troubleshooting Actions

When it comes to tackling issues in Sheets, there are a few fundamental troubleshooting steps that can often do the trick. Reloading the spreadsheet, opting for an alternative browser, or switching your Wi-Fi connection might just be the solution you need. If any of the aforementioned problems are causing you headaches, don't worry! I've got you covered with a set of handy solutions designed to help you troubleshoot and resolve them. Let's dive right in and get those sheets back on track!

9.2.1 Ensuring a Stable Internet Connection

To maximize your experience with Sheets, Google's cloud-based productivity tool, it's crucial to have a stable internet connection. While offline access is possible, certain features are only available when you're connected to the internet. If you encounter slow loading times or your spreadsheets fail to load altogether, take a moment to ensure the stability of your internet connection before taking further action.

To troubleshoot, begin by refreshing the page after confirming the stability of your internet connection. If the issue persists, consider switching to a different network or transitioning from a wireless to a cable connection. Additionally, if you've previously connected to the network using your phone, you can retrieve the Wi-Fi password.

It's worth noting that the quality of your connection may be impacted when multiple users are simultaneously connected to the same Wi-Fi network. In such cases, disconnecting other devices may help you work more efficiently in Sheets. Alternatively, repositioning your Wi-Fi router in an uncluttered area can reduce interference from electrical appliances, enhancing the signal quality.

When utilizing Sheets on your phone, try changing your physical location, as this simple adjustment can sometimes improve connectivity. As a last resort, if you frequently encounter difficulties connecting to Wi-Fi networks, resetting your network settings may provide a resolution.

9.2.2 Clearing Cookies and Cache

When using your browser, it's common for website data like HTML pages and images to be stored in a cache. This cache helps to improve your browsing experience by reducing bandwidth usage and speeding up server load times. Additionally, cookies are used to track your interactions with a website and store information such as passwords, browser history, and preferences.

However, there are times when updated website content can clash with the data stored in your cache and cookies, resulting in errors. If this happens, you can easily resolve the issue by clearing the cache and cookies in the Android app or web version of Sheets. It's advisable to start by clearing the cache and cookies for the web app alone. Clearing all cookies in your browser will remove login information and preferences for all websites you've visited.

9.2.3 Using a Different Web Browser

For optimal performance when using Google Sheets and other Workspace applications, it is recommended to choose from the following browsers: Chrome, Firefox, Microsoft Edge, and Safari. By utilizing any of these options, you can fully explore the extensive range of features offered. In the event that Sheets fails to function properly on your default browser, simply switch to another browser.

Moreover, it is crucial to enable cookies and JavaScript. Cookies ensure that you remain signed in to your accounts and retain your preferred settings. Meanwhile, JavaScript facilitates the seamless execution of dynamic interactions and features.

9.2.4 Getting Rid of Unwanted Access

Some time ago, the Verge encountered an unfortunate incident where their website downtime was inadvertently shared via Google Docs with unintended viewers. The oversight of neglecting to restrict access to view-only mode led to a flurry of comical annotations flooding the document.

To prevent such blunders, it's crucial to review the permissions of your spreadsheets before initiating collaboration or sharing them. If mishandled, individuals to whom you've granted ownership rights could tamper with permissions, potentially ejecting you from the document or even permanently erasing it. Safeguarding your files from such mishaps requires vigilance and attention to detail.

9.2.5 Clearing Chrome's Hosted App Data

Just like cookies and caches, hosted app data in Chrome refers to the information stored by extensions and apps from the Chrome Web Store in your browser when you download and use them. Sometimes, this data can cause conflicts with certain applications, like Sheets. In such cases, wiping the hosted app's data might be the solution when other troubleshooting methods fail. Here's how you can do it:

- Launch the Chrome app on your Chromebook, Windows computer, Mac, or phone.
- If you're using a Windows computer, hit the Ctrl+Shift+Delete keys to access the menu for clearing browsing data. Mac users need to use Command+Shift+Delete.
- Next, select the "Advanced" option.
- Pick the desired time range for which you want to clear the data.
- Proceed to the bottom of the page and locate the "Hosted app data" option. Make sure to untick the boxes for other items, like browsing history.
- Finally, select the "Clear data" option to remove the hosted app data from your Chrome browser.

9.2.6 Simplifying Your Spreadsheet for Improved Performance

When it comes to spreadsheets, bigger isn't always better. The more cells you have in your sheets, the slower it becomes, transforming simple calculations from seconds to minutes. However, there are ways to streamline your spreadsheet and make it run smoothly.

Start by trimming the fat. Delete unnecessary columns, rows, and cells to reduce the size of your spreadsheet. If you find that your data is overwhelming a single spreadsheet, consider migrating some entries to another one.

To avoid the tedious copy-and-paste method, give the IMPORTRANGE function a try. This handy function allows you to import data from one spreadsheet to another while keeping them in sync. This means that any changes made in one spreadsheet will automatically update the other.

To use IMPORTRANGE to copy data into a new spreadsheet, follow these steps:

- First, launch Google Sheets and open the spreadsheet that you would like to copy data from.
- Go to the address bar of your browser and copy the URL.
- Then, double-click a cell in the new spreadsheet and type =IMPORTRANGE without any spaces.
- After that, insert a bracket and open a quotation. Paste the copied URL and close the quotation mark, then insert a comma.
- Next, define the cell range you would like to import by opening another quotation and typing the name of the sheet, such as Sheet 3 or Sheet 4, followed by an exclamation mark and the cell range.
- Close the quotation and the function with a bracket, and hit the Enter key to execute the function.

Keep in mind that Sheets may show a #REF error the first time you import a spreadsheet, but you can resolve this by granting access to your account from the original spreadsheet.

9.2.7 Ensure your Google Workspace storage is Sufficient

When you set up a personal Google account, you are granted a default storage limit of 15GB. However, this storage is shared among Google Photos, Google Drive, Gmail, and all other Workspace applications. If you frequently back up documents and media content, this allocation may be insufficient.

In the event that your storage reaches its capacity, you will be unable to access existing files in Sheets or create new ones. To address this issue, Google offers the option to upgrade your storage to a maximum of two terabytes by subscribing to a Google One membership plan.

9.2.8 Creating a Copy

Creating a duplicate of a Google spreadsheet comes in handy when you encounter stubborn ones that refuse to open. By making a copy, you can easily pick up where you left off on the fresh version, while the original remains intact unless you choose to delete it.

Unfortunately, browsers don't offer a straightforward way to duplicate spreadsheets from the Sheets home menu. However, you can easily accomplish this on the mobile app, which provides the necessary option. Remember, Sheets doesn't support making multiple copies simultaneously, so you'll have to repeat the process each time you want to duplicate a spreadsheet.

- To get started, launch the Google Sheets app and locate the three-dot icon adjacent to the desired spreadsheet.

- Tap on it and choose the "Make a copy" option.
- Next, add a title to the document and choose the desired folder that you would like to save it in.
- Once done, tap "OK" to initiate the duplication.

Sheets will automatically open the newly created copy, allowing you to resume your editing tasks without stress.

Conclusion

Google Sheets has quickly proven itself as a useful resource for individuals as well as businesses. It is an indispensable part of the Google Workspace suite due to its adaptability, usability, and collaboration features. As was mentioned, there are many different functions, formulas, and formatting options available in Sheets, enabling users to easily do sophisticated math operations and data analysis. Additionally, it allows for seamless team collaboration in real-time, increasing productivity and efficiency.

The utility and usefulness of Google Sheets are further increased by the connection of Google Sheets with other Google Workspace programs like Google Docs and Google Slides. Sheets is flexible enough to adapt to diverse processes and requirements thanks to its ability to import data from other sources and export to a variety of file formats. Additionally, users are able to customize Sheets to their specific needs thanks to the addition of add-ons and templates, significantly enhancing its functionality.

Additionally, Google Sheets' cloud-based architecture makes it possible for users to access their spreadsheets on any device and from any location without the hassle of installing or updating the software. Because of this accessibility and features like automatic saving and revision history, there is no need to worry about data loss.

To sum up, Google Sheets has completely changed how individuals and organizations manage spreadsheets and data analysis. It is an essential tool for productivity and efficiency thanks to its user-friendly interface, wide range of functionality, and interactive features. Google Sheets' capabilities will probably keep getting better as technology develops, further confirming its status as the industry's best spreadsheet program.

END

Thank you for reading my book.

Tim A. Kirksey

Made in the USA
Las Vegas, NV
09 November 2023

80533828R00098